Severn
Valley Steam

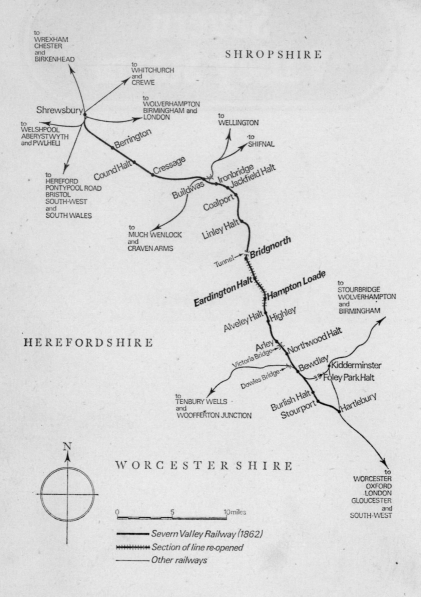

to
WREXHAM
CHESTER
and
BIRKENHEAD

to
WHITCHURCH
and
CREWE

SHROPSHIRE

to
WOLVERHAMPTON
BIRMINGHAM and
LONDON

Shrewsbury

to
WELLINGTON

to
WELSHPOOL
ABERYSTWYTH
and PWLHELI

Berrington

·to
SHIFNAL

to
HEREFORD
PONTYPOOL ROAD
BRISTOL
SOUTH-WEST
and
SOUTH WALES

Cound Halt

Cressage

Ironbridge

Jackfield Halt

Buildwas

Coalport

to
MUCH WENLOCK
and
CRAVEN ARMS

Linley Halt

Tunnel

Bridgnorth

to
STOURBRIDGE
WOLVERHAMPTON
and
BIRMINGHAM

Eardington Halt

Hampton Loade

HEREFORDSHIRE

Alveley Halt

Highley

Northwood Halt

Arley

Victoria Bridge

Bewdley

Kidderminster

Dowles Bridge

Foley Park Halt

to
TENBURY WELLS
and
WOOFFERTON JUNCTION

Burlish Halt

Stourport

Hartlebury

N

WORCESTERSHIRE

to
WORCESTER
OXFORD
LONDON
GLOUCESTER
and
SOUTH-WEST

0   5   10 miles

Severn Valley Railway (1862)
Section of line re-opened
Other railways

Severn Valley Railway

Severn Valley Steam

Sir Gerald Nabarro

Routledge & Kegan Paul London

First published 1971
by Routledge & Kegan Paul Ltd
Broadway House, 68–74 Carter Lane,
London EC4V 5EL
Printed in Great Britain by
The Camelot Press Ltd,
London and Southampton
and set in 10 on 12 pt Old Style
© Sir Gerald Nabarro 1971

ISBN 0 7100 7064 0 (c)
ISBN 0 7100 7069 1 (p)

Contents

v

Illustrations

Illustrations between pages 12 and 13

The seal of the Severn Valley Railway Company
(By permission of the Curator of Historical Relics of the British Railways Board)

Severn Valley tickets; Iron Bridge & Broseley station
(By permission of the Curator of Historical Relics of the British Railways Board, the Severn Valley Railway Co. and Locomotive & General Railway Photographs)

Sir Morton Peto; Sir John Fowler; Isambard Kingdom Brunel; Sir Daniel Gooch
(By permission of the Institution of Civil Engineers, London; the Science Museum, London; the Curator of Historical Relics of the British Railways Board and BR Western Region)

The Clarkson steam bus
(By permission of W. E. Rutter, Esq.)

The Rt Hon. George Cecil Weld Forester
(By permission of the Wolverhampton Hospital Management Committee)

'The gay nineties'; a Sunday school outing, c. 1896
(By permission of the Borough Librarian, Kidderminster)

Neen Sollars station, *c.* 1900; 'Sunday best at Kidderminster', *c.* 1896
(By permission of the Borough Librarian, Kidderminster)

Bewdley station, *c.* 1910
(By permission of J. Francis Parker, Esq.)

322 class no. 338 shunting at Bewdley, *c.* 1925
(By permission of J. Francis Parker, Esq.)

3232 class no. 3244 leaving Bewdley
(By permission of J. Francis Parker, Esq.)

455 class tank no. 976 at Kidderminster station, *c.* 1920
(By permission of J. Francis Parker, Esq.)

Side tank no. 18 at Bewdley, *c.* 1925
(By permission of J. Francis Parker, Esq.)

Pannier tank no. 325 at Stourbridge Junction, *c.* 1924
(By permission of J. Francis Parker, Esq.)

Pannier tank of the 1076 or Buffalo class entering Kidderminster,
c. 1925
(By permission of J. Francis Parker, Esq.)

Buildwas station in 1932
(By permission of Locomotive & General Railway Photographs)

Sir Gerald Nabarro, M.P., on ex-GWR Collett goods no. 3205 at
Bridgnorth, 1970
(Photographer G. C. Lees, Esq.)

Illustrations between pages 28 and 29

Pioneer BR standard class 3 tank no. 82000 approaches Bewdley,
early 1960s

Buildwas station, Severn Valley platform, 1932; Sir Gerald Nabarro,
M.P., on footplate of ex-GWR Collett goods no. 3205, 1970
(By permission of G. C. Lees, Esq. and Locomotive & General
Railway Photographs)

Ex-GWR diesel railcar no. 26 at Hartlebury, Worcestershire, 1959;
ex-GWR 61XX large Prairie tank no. 6118 at Stourport-on-Severn,
1957
(Photographer M. Hale, Esq.)

Ex-LMS (Crab) no. 42783 entering Bewdley station, 1960
(Photographer D. A. Johnson, Esq.)

43XX Mogul no. 6314 hauling coal in the cutting between Northwood
Halt and Bewdley, 1963
(Photographer B. S. Moore, Esq.)

GWR diesel railcar on the Dowles Bridge, c. 1946

Ex-GWR pannier tank no. 9656 at Northwood Halt, 1961
(Photographer E. J. Dew, Esq.)

Ex-GWR pannier tank no. 3619 in 1962
(Photographer R. J. Sellick, Esq.)

The last scheduled passenger train leaving Bridgnorth, 8 September
1962
(Photographer E. J. Dew, Esq.)

Ex-GWR 55XX no. 5518 stopping at Coalport, 1957; ex-GWR 41XX
class passes Coalport, 1962
(Photographers M. Hale, Esq. and R. W. Tennent, Esq.)

Railcar no. 29 and ex-GWR no. 9639 at Buildwas Junction, 1959;
Ivatt 2-6-2 BR tank no. 41240 at Courd Halt, 1963; ex-GWR
no. 5555 at Shrewsbury, 1961
(Photographers M. Hale, Esq., R. J. Sellick, Esq. and E. J. Dow
Esq.)

Coalport station, looking towards Bewdley, in 1932
(By permission of Locomotive & General Railway Photographs)

Ex-GWR 0-6-0 no. 3205 at Bridgnorth in 1967
(Photographer D. C. Williams, Esq.)

'Gardeners' delight' – the line between Hampton Loade and Alveley
in 1967
(Photographer D. C. Williams, Esq.)

'Contemporary steam' – ex-LMSR Ivatt no. 46443 and ex-GWR
Collett no. 3205, 1967
(Photographer D. C. Williams, Esq.)

No. 3205 hauls a 'special' in 1968 and a train from Bridgnorth to
Hampton Loade in 1970
(Photographers T. Stephens, Esq. and J. R. P. Hunt, Esq.)

Illustrations between pages 44 and 45

No. 3205 at Bridgnorth in 1970, with Ivatt no. 46443 awaiting
departure
(By permission of the *Express and Star*, Wolverhampton)

Z15, a six coach BR 'special' hauled by no. 3205, leaving Bridgnorth,
1970
(Photographer J. D. Montgomery, Esq.)

'Preservationists' delight' – ex-LMSR no. 46443 at Knowle Sands in
1967, and surrounded by hundreds of fans
(Photographer D. C. Williams, Esq.)

No. 46443 leaves Hampton Loade bound for Bridgnorth, 1970
(Photographer D. C. Williams, Esq.)

No. 46443 at Hay bridge, Eardington in 1970
(Photographer A. G. Cattle, Esq.)

'Britannia' – ex-BR no. 70000 – now operating on the Severn Valley
line
(By permission of the British Railways Board)

Ex-LMSR Ivatt class 4 no. 43106 passing Hampton Loade, 1968;
no. 43106 leaving Bridgnorth, 1970
(Photographers D. C. Williams, Esq. and A. G. Cattle, Esq.)

No. 43106 at Oldbury Grange, 1970
(Photographer D. C. Williams, Esq.)

'Steam to spare' – no. 43106 in 1970
(Photographer A. G. Cattle, Esq.)

Diesel railcar no. 22, owned by Western Preservations Ltd
(Photographer D. A. Johnson, Esq.)

Ex-LMSR locomotives now in service with the Severn Valley line
(By permission of the 8F Locomotive Society)

No. 8233 crossing the Victoria bridge, 1970
(Photographer A. G. Cattle, Esq.)

Illustrations

No. 8233 at work in 1970: leaving Bridgnorth; near Eardingon; at Oldbury Grange
(Photographers J. B. Hicks, Esq., J. R. Whitman, Esq. and D. C. Williams, Esq.)

'Under starter's orders' at Bridgnorth, 1970
(Photographer D. C. Williams, Esq.)

Ex-GWR tank no. 4566 in BR livery being restored at Bewdley
(Photographer P. W. Gray, Esq.)

'R.A.F. Biggin Hill' – Stanier class 5, no. 45110: double-heads no. 44949 at Whaley bridge, 1968; now owned by the Flairavia Flying Club, on the Severn Valley line, 1970
(Photographers J. Lacey, Esq. and D. C. Williams, Esq.)

Illustrations between pages 92 and 93

Ex-LMS no. 7383 'Jinty' tank no. 47383, now owned by the Manchester Rail Travel Society: on the M1 motorway in 1968; shunting in the Williamsthorpe colliery sidings, 1967
(Photographer D. C. Williams, Esq.)

Ex-GWR 1500 class shunting engines: no. 1501, owned by the Warwickshire Industrial Locomotive Preservation Group, at Bridgnorth; no. 1500 at Swindon in 1949
(By permission of the Warwickshire Preservationists and the Curator of Historical Relics of the British Railways Board)

'Warwickshire', a Manning Wardle saddle tank owned by the Warwickshire Industrial Locomotive Preservation Group, in 1970: after naming at Bridgnorth; crossing Oldbury viaduct
(Photographers B. S. Moore, Esq. and D. C. Williams, Esq.)

'The Lady Armaghdale', a Hunslet side tank, no. 686, now owned by the Warwickshire Industrial Locomotive Preservation Group, in 1970: at Bridgnorth; at Oldbury Grange
(Photographers B. S. Moore, Esq. and D. C. Williams, Esq.)

Nigel Gresley A3 Pacific, 'Mallard', BR no. 60022, formerly LNER no. 4468, now in the Clapham Railway Museum: on the Leeds–London express, 1964; on the Tees–Tyne Pullman, 1965
(Photographer the Rt Rev. Eric Treacy, Bishop of Wakefield)

Illustrations

Bridgnorth station: *c.* 1863, from the Castle; *c.* 1890, from Pudding Hill
(Derived from contemporary pictures)

Evesham dinner 1 May 1852
(From the *Illustrated London News*)

Pub sign at Evesham
(By permission of the *Evesham Journal and Four Shires Advertiser*)

North Yorkshire Moors Railway open weekend at Goathland station; tank engines at Croes Newydd for the Dart Valley Railway
(Photographers John M. Boyes, Esq. and I. H. Waite, Esq.)

'Dukedog' at Sheffield Park on the Bluebell line; 'Union of South Africa' at Lochty
(Photographers J. H. Waite, Esq. and John B. Cameron, Esq.)

Locomotives on the Keighley & Worth Valley Railway
(Photographers D. N. Scott, Esq. and J. Binks, Esq.)

'Great Western Glory', no. 5786, and 'King George V' at Hereford
(By permission of the Worcester Locomotive Society)

The Vale of Rheidol Railway
(By permission of British Railways)

Locomotives on the Dart Valley Railway
(By permission of the Dart Valley Railway Co. Ltd and John M. Boyes, Esq.)

Welshpool & Llanfair Light Railway – 'Sir Drefaldwyn'
(Photographer R. L. Cartwright, Esq.)

Talyllyn Railway, 'Dolgoch', and Festiniog Railway, 'Earl of Merioneth'
(Photographers J. F. Rimmer, Esq. and A. Heywood, Esq.)

Foreword

I am delighted to write this foreword for the splendid book on the Severn Valley Railway by Sir Gerald Nabarro M.P., who has been intimately concerned with the public and political life of Worcestershire since 1945. He has an unparalleled knowledge of the country through which this railway was built and of the economic and tourist importance of so many places between Worcester and Shrewsbury. The valley has outstanding natural beauty and two thousand years of recorded history since Uriconium was established in Roman times.

Though the Severn Valley Railway virtually shut down in 1963 under the Beeching closures after 100 years of operation, the recent resuscitation by a private company, of which I am happy to be President, offers most exciting prospects. By 1971 the company had secured full ownership of the section of the line between Bridgnorth and Hampton Loade operated entirely by steam locomotives, and hopes to operate the entire length of line to Kidderminster shortly. This will undoubtedly be a major tourist attraction and a magnet for

steam locomotive lovers from all parts of Britain and from overseas: the history of the Severn Valley Railway, contemporary operations on the line with steam traction, and future prospects are all related, accompanied by copious photography, in Sir Gerald's book, *Severn Valley Steam*.

I hope that this important contribution to railway history and chronicles will meet with the success it richly deserves.

Cobham

Hagley Hall,
Worcestershire

Preface

I have been interested in railways all my life and I retain a particular affection for the Great Western, having been reared to the age of fourteen close to the main line a few miles west of Paddington. My association with the Severn Valley line, which was finally absorbed by the GWR in 1872, also goes back to my boyhood. I first travelled on it in the year of the General Strike. The ride behind a Dean goods, which I remember for its double frame and splendid condition, though it was forty years old, made a lasting impression on me and I hoped that the newly introduced Castle class of locomotive would eventually include engines named after the castles in the Severn valley at Shrewsbury, Bridgnorth, Arley and Hartlebury.

My connection with the line became more permanent twenty years later when I was adopted as prospective Conservative candidate for Kidderminster, which included the southern half of the line and had been formed from some part of the Bewdley division of Worcestershire, formerly represented by Stanley Baldwin who, like his father, had been a director of the GWR and whose uncles Pearce, William and Enoch, as the following pages describe, were closely concerned with the origins of the Severn Valley Railway. In 1950 I was helped in my General Election campaign, conducted from the George Hotel at Bewdley, by Sir Francis Winnington, great-grandson of Sir Thomas Winnington who had presided at the 'Railway Dinner' in the same hotel in 1862. Towards the end of my fifteen years as M.P. for Kidderminster I was active in the fight to save the line from closure under the Transport Act of 1962, following the Beeching Report.

Since 1966, as M.P. for South Worcestershire – which included the south and west parts of the old Bewdley constituency – and much more recently as a director of the present Severn Valley Railway Co., my association with the area and the line has remained unbroken.

I do not feel that any further justification is necessary for my authorship of this book. Over the years I had acquired a great deal of information about the line but it has been vastly increased in preparing the book by consultations with many archivists and railway historians for whose co-operation I wish to record my warmest gratitude: the British Railways Board Archivist and his staff; the Clerk of the Records, House of Lords, and his staff; the Research Librarian, House of Commons, and his staff; the Curator of Historical Relics, B.R.B.; the County Archivists of Shropshire and Worcestershire; the City Librarian of Worcester and the Borough Librarians of Kidderminster and Shrewsbury; the Librarian of the Institution of Civil Engineers; the Public Relations Department of British Railways, Western Region; Mr C. W. Clarke, Editor of the *Evesham Journal and Four Shires Advertiser*; Mr J. Francis Parker; Mr John Bonham-Carter, Chairman and General Manager of the Western Region of British Railways; Mr Patrick Garland, a director of the Talyllyn Railway Co. and the Dart Valley Railway Co.; Mr. Richard Dunn, a director of the Severn Valley Railway Co.; Lord Forester; and Mr F. C. Perrett. I have also had the benefit of the unrivalled expertise of Mr C. R. Clinker and Mr O. S. Nock on railway and locomotive history respectively. I also wish to thank my own research team: Mr T. F. O'Sullivan, Mr Neil Sinclair, Mr David Williams and Mrs Margaret Mason.

The photographs in this book have been widely admired and I want particularly to thank my constituents, Mr and Mrs John Beckerley of Hanley Swan, near Worcester, who have travelled widely collecting material and have prepared prints and photographs of all ages and conditions for publication with the greatest skill and enthusiasm.

I have co-operated in Worcestershire affairs for twenty-five years with my friend Lord Cobham, and I am grateful to him as a lover of steam engines and railways for providing the Foreword.

Finally, I congratulate the publishers on a rapid and most attractive production.

My personal wish, as a director of the Severn Valley Railway Co., is to recreate the railway from Bridgnorth to Kidderminster, fully operational by steam traction throughout, as a major attraction for enthusiasts from all over the world, a splendid touristic enterprise and a singularly appropriate historical asset in an area of Britain which was the cradle of the first industrial revolution. I hope this book will be a contribution towards all these important objectives.

Gerald Nabarro

House of Commons

Acknowledgments

The author wishes to express his thanks to the directors, staff and members of the Severn Valley Railway for their help in the preparation of the text and photographs of this book; to Mr C. R. Clinker for preparing the tables of mileages and traffic figures and to Mr D. C. Williams for preparing the table of locomotive specifications.

1
The Age of Steam

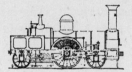

This is a book about the Severn Valley Railway in Worcestershire and Shropshire, opened in 1862. The line was conceived in the years of railway mania when hundreds of promotions, inspired by the success of the Stockton & Darlington Railway, opened in 1825, and the Liverpool & Manchester Railway, opened in 1830, were presented to Parliament for approval.

By the 1840s the first phase of the industrial revolution was over and the main period of railway building came at the beginning of a period of social and industrial consolidation. There were a good many casualties among the offspring of the mania and Westminster was littered with their corpses: some of the schemes were abandoned when it became apparent that they were fundamentally unrealistic, others were simply rejected by Parliament. Still more were victims of the vicissitudes of opinion in the areas for which they were planned, among them the earliest schemes for the Severn Valley. Those enterprises that survived to be built and operated, whether independently or in amalgamation with others, mostly developed into efficient and viable railways. The profit motive and test of profitability in Victorian times were hard but fair arbiters.

The Reform Act of 1832 had enfranchised millions of new voters in the rapidly-growing industrial communities of Britain. The long reign of Queen Victoria, which began at the same time as the building of the Great Western Railway in 1837, was a period of great improvement in communications.

Transport by rail all over the country was becoming more widely accepted if not entirely safe, and, by our standards, certainly not comfortable. Nevertheless, the advantages of travel in the wooden four-wheeler carriages, running on crude metal rails, over the discomforts and hazards of the stage-coach or long, wearying miles on horseback and on foot, quickly became apparent. Though the clanking early monsters through the meadows might scare the cattle, rouse the landowners to demoniac opposition and quicken the processes of democracy by encouraging cheap and relatively rapid travel for the masses of industrial workers, railways were accepted as an essential and imperative accompaniment of dynamic industrialization.

Topographically, it was usually economical and logical to build railways along the valleys of rivers. This was evident from lines all over Britain. The proposition was not slow to gain recognition early in the days of railway mania in its application to Britain's greatest natural waterway, the Severn. Thus, there was born the idea, at about the time of Victoria's accession, of a railway along the Severn valley, from the ancient town of Shrewsbury to the royal city of Worcester. It would run impressively and profitably through the land of the Lords Marchers, following rather closely the river itself, avoiding as far as possible those areas most liable to flooding.

The origin of the name Severn is more exotic than that of any other English river. The Latin name 'Sabrina' as the writings of Tacitus and other historians of Roman Britain show, has a long and respectable history, but it originated a thousand years before that. According to the *Historia Regum Britanniae*, an account of the kings who dwelt in Britain before the incarnation of Christ written by the twelfth-century monk and bishop of St Asaph, Geoffrey of Monmouth, Estrildis, a German maiden brought to Britain by King Humber, was loved by Locrine and was the mother by him of Sabrina; but Locrine's real wife, Gwendolen, was so enraged by this that she caused both Estrildis and her daughter to be drowned in the river, whereafter, continues Geoffrey:

> Gwendolen published an edict through all Britain, that the river should bear the damsel's name, hoping by this to perpetuate her memory, and by that the infamy of her husband. So that to this day the river is called in the British tongue Sabren, which by the corruption of the name is in another language Sabrina.
> Geoffrey of Monmouth (trs. Lewis Thorpe), *History of the Kings of Britain* (Penguin)

2

The legend has been used or repeated by many poets, among them
Spenser and Swinburne, but above all by Milton in *Comus*, a pastoral
entertainment dedicated to the Earl of Bridgewater, Lord President
of Wales, and first presented at Ludlow Castle in 1634:

> There is a gentle Nymph not far from hence,
> That with moist curb sways the smooth Severn stream,
> Sabrina is her name, a Virgin pure,
> Whilom she was the daughter of Locrine,
> That had the Sceptre from his father Brute.
> The guiltless damsel flying the mad pursuit
> Of her enraged stepdam Gwendolen,
> Commended her fair innocence to the flood
> That stay'd her flight with his cross-flowing course,
> The water Nymphs that in the bottom played,
> Held up their pearled writs and took her in,
> Bearing her straight to aged Nero's hall,
> Who piteous of her woes, rear'd her lank head,
> And gave him to his daughters to imbathe
> In nectar'd lavers strew'd with Asphodil,
> And through the porch and inlet of each sense
> Dropped in Ambrosial oils till she reviv'd,
> And underwent a quick immortal change,
> Made Goddess of the River . . .

From its rising on the long slope of Plynlimon in the mountains of
central Wales, the river, under the Welsh name of Hafryn, flows by
the towns of Llanidloes and Montgomery, where the Norman castle
dominates the stream; thence into England by Shrewsbury, where
the Severn valley is generally regarded as beginning. It was where
the Severn Valley Railway was to begin too, following southward the
course of the valley to Bridgnorth and Bewdley and eventually to
Stourport-on-Severn and Hartlebury, close to the flourishing city of
Worcester.

Thus the early Victorians conceived of the railway and, noting
that it might cut off a considerable distance from the comparatively
circuitous route between Worcester and Shrewsbury via Hartlebury,
Kidderminster, Stourbridge, Wolverhampton and Wellington,
regarded it as a promising enterprise. The East Shropshire coalfield
around Coalbrookdale, Buildwas, Broseley, Ironbridge, Coalport,
together with the iron mines around Wellington, was the first centre
of industrial development in the north Midlands. As well as the old

road and river routes, at Shrewsbury railways early developed towards Hereford in a south-westerly direction, towards Crewe and industrial south Lancashire, including Manchester and Liverpool in the north-east, towards Chester and the Dee estuary to the north, towards Welshpool in the west and Wolverhampton in the south-east: all these routes converged on Shrewsbury in a disorderly splurge of warring companies and interests. Shrewsbury was the node, just as Worcester was to become the centre of another complex fifty miles to the south. The GWR had reached Didcot, 53 miles from Paddington, and continued to Oxford. Thence the trouble-prone project, the Oxford, Worcester & Wolverhampton Railway, was eventually to take a main-line service on to Wolverhampton. From Worcester, other companies linked up with Hereford, Gloucester and Cheltenham, and thence to Bristol, and in the other direction with Birmingham.

Thus Shrewsbury and Worcester both provided splendid traffic outlets and connections for the proposed Severn Valley line. Fourteen miles from Worcester was the flourishing woollen textile town of Kidderminster, with the inland port of Stourport-on-Severn near by at the western end of Brindley's 'stinking ditch' – the Staffordshire and Worcestershire Canal. Further north at Bewdley, there was a major crossing of the Severn by Telford's bridge, completed in 1798. This great engineer built the bridge and the toll house by it in one year. Sadly, the toll house was removed a few years ago in spite of vigorous efforts to save it by the Bewdley Civic Society. He built his bridge in stone quarried at Arley, four miles to the north, and himself described it as magnificent. Arley stone has a very distinctive and satisfying colour and although most of Bewdley was rebuilt in the days of its greatest prosperity in the seventeenth and early eighteenth centuries in the then fashionable brick, it was the colour of the stone in which the earlier town was constructed that the antiquary and topographer John Leland was most struck by when he visited Bewdley in about 1540:

> The towne of Bewdley is sett on the side of a hille, so comely that a man cannot wishe to see a towne better. It riseth from the Severne banke by east, upon the hille by west, so that a man standing upon the hille trans pontem by east may discern almost every house in the towne; and att the rising of the sun from east, the whole towne glittereth, being all of new building, as it were of gould.

4

The railway would go on north to Arley itself, lying astride the river only connected by ferry. It was on the route of the proposed railway and just north of the only one of four intended crossings of the river which the Severn Valley Railway Co. actually carried out. Then through an outlying part of the Shropshire coalfield around Highley and Alveley which would ensure valuable mineral traffic for the line, and then back into the more characteristically lush meadows of the valley around Hampton Loade and Eardington. At Bridgnorth another Telford bridge crosses the Severn, one of more than forty he built in the last decade of the eighteenth century, including those at Buildwas and Bewdley. Here the railway would encounter its second greatest obstacle – after the river itself – in the shape of the great cliff towering over the town and formerly crowned by a castle, one of the strongholds of the Marches. Telford also built the church of St Mary Magdalene in the High Town and this building, together with the castle ruins, appears in the background of several of the illustrations in this book.

The area has many historical associations with steam traction. As early as 1802 the Cornish mine captain and engineer Richard Trevithick built an engine which operated at Coalbrookdale. This second steam engine designed and built by Trevithick had a cast-iron boiler $1\frac{1}{2}$ inches thick (with an interior wrought iron tube) and was 48 inches in diameter and 72 inches long. The cylinder was 7 inches in diameter with a stroke of 36 inches.

All the great railway trunk routes originated a few years before the Severn Valley line. By 1840, within only fifteen years of the opening of the Stockton & Darlington line in 1825, London had been connected by main-line trunk routes to Bristol, Southampton, Birmingham, Liverpool and Manchester. It was a prodigious performance, executed by masses of navvies, mostly Irish, working without bulldozers, earth movers, tippers, the mechanical shovel or indeed any tools other than cart, wheelbarrow, pick and shovel.

But progress elsewhere was slow. The Eastern Counties (later a constituent of the Great Eastern) was only seventeen miles out of London; the Great Northern's main line from King's Cross to Peterborough, Grantham and Doncaster did not open until 1852; the Midland Counties Railway (soon to join other companies as the Midland) groped its way south, first to Rugby and its London terminus at Euston Square, then to Hitchin (en route to King's Cross) and finally to St Pancras in 1868, whence its trunk routes stretched northward to Leicester, Nottingham, Derby, Sheffield,

5

Leeds, Bradford and Carlisle. Not to be outdone, the mighty London & North Western Railway, self-styled 'Premier Line', formed in 1846 by amalgamation of the London & Birmingham, Grand Junction and Manchester & Birmingham Railways, eventually reached such outposts as Abergavenny, Newport, Cardiff, Merthyr, Swansea and even Carmarthen, challenging the hegemony of the Great Western and its associates in the lush and rewarding traffic of the South Wales coalfields.

In Scotland the North British carried the east coast route to Edinburgh, and the Caledonian & Glasgow and South Western Companies promoted the traffic from the west coast route and the LNWR into Glasgow and central Scotland then on to Aberdeen. The Highland Railway and the Great North of Scotland companies gave access to Perth, Inverness and the far north, to Wick and Thurso, and to the west Highland centres of Fort William and Mallaig.

Within thirty years of the mania of the 1840s, scores of smaller companies had been gobbled up by their neighbours, amalgamated, taken over, or closed through financial failure. In the process, the railway war was waged with a ferocity unknown even in our most sensational take-over bids, company amalgamations and acquisitions of today. Generally, though, it was good business and most of the principal lines emerging at the turn of the century were successful, enterprising and efficient, rewarding to their stockholders and blue chips in the investment world.

The arrival of the motor vehicle changed all that in the twentieth century. The Great War and road competition led to government-sponsored grouping of railways in Britain very soon after the 1918 Armistice. The ravages of war had been immense and the railway companies emerged after their titanic war efforts in varying stages of disrepair but with one feature in common, an immense backlog of maintenance to be made good for locomotives and rolling stock, permanent way and signalling, stations, depots, docks and harbours. In addition, government control of railways and ancillary services during the four and a quarter years of war had demonstrated even to the most bigoted and dogmatic of free enterprise railways that co-ordination in the public and national interest brought advantage to both strong and weak railway companies.

Parliament in 1922 took the first step towards nationalization, which was to come finally in 1947. Basically, this measure formed the railways of Britain into four major groups based on principles of affinities between companies, geographical location and coverage. This was the prelude to the nationalization of the railways which followed World War II, and the creation of British Railways, a single state-owned railways monopoly, now nearly twenty-five years old.

In 1947 by a major enactment of a socialist government the era of the railway companies ended on the creation of a British Transport Commision. About 20,000 miles of route, and rising three quarters of a million railway and allied workers were nationalized. The painful processes of coagulation into a single public service had begun. It is no part of my narrative to survey the history of nationalization, for better or worse, since 1947.

Steam traction came to an end on British Railways in 1968, after 138 years of railway history since the 'Rocket' of 1830, and steam locomotives were all replaced by the now familiar diesel and electric engines and traction throughout Britain, except on the steam preservation railways.

Steam-hauled trains have been reborn, and the preservation railway lines founded, under Ministry of Transport Light Railway Orders. These include, operating ex-BR steam locomotives and stock, such famous enterprises as the Severn Valley Railway, the Bluebell line, the Keighley & Worth Valley Railway and the Dart Valley Railway, all in standard 4 feet 8½ inches gauge, and no doubt many more will follow. There are also numerous narrow-gauge railways operated with steam engines, such as the 'little railways of Wales' (the Tallylyn, Welshpool & Llanfair and the Festiniog) and the Vale of Rheidol Railway owned and operated by BR, the Romney, Hythe & Dymchurch and the Ravenglass & Eskdale Railways. Altogether, hundreds of steam locomotives have been saved from breakers' yards.

Private owners everywhere are seeking facilities to steam and to operate many of these priceless preserved engines, the majority in standard gauge, on the resuscitated lines. A leader here is the Severn Valley Co., fully operational from 1862 to 1963, then for mineral and freight traffic only on a declining scale until 1970 when the line was finally closed. During this run-down the new Severn Valley Railway was founded and all the contemporary pictures in this book give testimony to the admirable progress achieved since the new company began operations in 1967. It is the essence of the steam engine revival, and characterizes the preservation movement all over Britain.

Of course, they are the steam locomotives which 'send' the fans.

The station architecture, the permanent way, the signalling arrangements and the remaining railway paraphernalia are interesting, essential and objective, but the engines are the centre-pieces and the true justification for preservation movements and societies in the railway world. Engines, their performance, speed, reliability, idiosyncrasies and every characteristic of all the diverse types and specifications since 'Locomotion', the first engine to run on a public railway (the Stockton & Darlington), down to the last steam locomotive to be built for British Railways, the 92XXX 9F class no. 92220, 2-10-0 wheel arrangement, 'Evening Star'. The 'Locomotion' was built by Stephenson & Co.

At the Rainhill trials in 1829 the Stephensons and Booth won the prize of £500 offered by the Liverpool & Manchester Railway competition and on her first twenty runs on the 1½-mile course at Rainhill, the 'Rocket' averaged 13.42 m.p.h. and achieved a maximum of 24.43 m.p.h. She had a white chimney and was painted yellow and black. In June 1841 an early Great Western train, forerunner of the 'Bristolian', travelled from Paddington to Temple Meads in 4 hours at a speed of slightly below 30 m.p.h.; and on an early through train from London to Yarmouth, on the Eastern Counties line, accomplished the 146 miles in 6¼ hours, at just over 22 m.p.h. The importance of these figures is to demonstrate developing speed, over substantial distances and with scheduled regularity, though not always punctuality. In 1840 'Firefly', a broad-gauge engine on the Great Western main line, ran from Paddington to Reading with forty passengers in 46¼ minutes at an average speed of approximately 47 m.p.h., and on the return trip the average speed between Twyford and Paddington was 50 m.p.h. for the 31 miles; the news of the accouchement of Queen Victoria was brought by special messenger on one of these GWR 2-2-2 broad-gauge engines from Slough to Paddington, 18¼ miles in 15 minutes 10 seconds or approximately 72 m.p.h. Speeds were climbing indeed, from the 'Rocket's' 13.42 m.p.h. in 1829 to 72 m.p.h. in 1844. In just fourteen years of steam locomotion, speed had multiplied five-fold. It continued, and in the year of the Great Exhibition a Crampton-type locomotive built for the South Eastern Railway achieved Redhill to Tonbridge (19 miles 47 chains) in 19½ minutes and Tonbridge to Ashford (26 miles 45 chains) in 20½ minutes, an average of 78 m.p.h.

The year 1870 saw a great advance in locomotive design and performance for long-distance trains. Patrick Stirling, locomotive superintendent of the Great Northern Railway, produced his classic

8 feet 1 inch single no. 1, a locomotive of 4-2-2 wheel arrangement characterized by great beauty and simplicity of design. The performance of these 'Stirling Singles' was outstandingly consistent in their day, the 1870s and 1880s, as the high scheduled speeds of the expresses on the Great Northern testify. The eight expresses a day, running non-stop to Grantham from King's Cross, a distance of 105¼ miles in 119 minutes down and 117 minutes up, with exemplary time-keeping, demonstrated how marvellously locomotive design had improved in four short decades since the Rainhill trials.

The lure of speed under steam did not desert the public mind. Speeds scheduled on the main line were now reaching nearly a mile a minute and 75 and 80 miles an hour maxima characterized the top expresses at the turn of the century.

The Great Western had launched their famous generation of four-coupled, inside-cylinder, double-framed, 4-4-0 wheel arrangement main-line engines: the 'Dukes' (the Bluebell line in Sussex has a splendid 'Dukedog', ex-Great Western engine, fully operational today), the 'Flowers', the 'Bulldogs' and the 'Cities', these latter engines assuming responsibility for many of the main-line trains. It was a 'City', namely 'City of Truro', which was generally credited with the world record under steam, about 102 m.p.h. down Wellington Bank in Somerset in 1904, which remained the record until one of Sir Nigel Gresley's 'Pacifics' seized it in the thirties.

Today, a generation grows up which has seen steam engines only 'on the box' or at the cinema. The steam preservation lines are the only opportunity the members of this generation will have to enjoy the exquisite experience of a ride on a steam-hauled train. The older generation which grew up with steam may indulge their nostalgia by visiting the preservation steam railways, especially the Severn Valley, which caters especially for the tourist trade and those who seek to explore the country of the Lords Marchers. All of English history from the Romans to the second Elizabethans has marched through this land, and the history of the Severn Valley Railway matches it, in absorbing and complementary fascination.

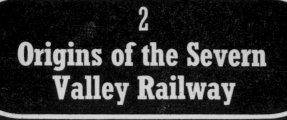

2
Origins of the Severn Valley Railway

Probably the first concrete plans for a direct railway link between Worcester and Shrewsbury were those of the Oxford, Worcester & Wolverhampton Railway, the 'Old Worse and Worse'. 'The initials alone', wrote Hamilton Ellis, 'of the Oxford, Worcester and Wolverhampton Railway, asked for such a nickname, but the company did its very best to live up to its courtesy title' (*British Railway History*, Allen & Unwin, 1954, vol. 1, p. 212).

The OW&W was planned partly as an attempt to extend and entrench the broad gauge, and thus also the position of the Great Western Railway, in the potentially lucrative west Midlands where it would operate in exhilarating proximity to its great rival, the London & North Western Railway. The proposal was immediately countered by the London and Birmingham Railway's plan for a line leaving its existing route at Tring, to run through Aylesbury and Banbury, to Evesham, Worcester, Stourport, Dudley and Wolverhampton, under the name of the London, Worcester & South Staffordshire Railway. As a standard – or, as it should more properly be called until the resolution of the gauge conflict – narrow-gauge enterprise, the London & Birmingham's plan naturally commended itself to the five railway 'Kings' – Lord Dalhousie, General Pasley, Captain O'Brien and Messrs Laing and Porter – who went to some lengths to prove that the broad gauge in general and the plans of the OW&W in particular were unworkable and unsafe. With the Great Western as its patron, however, the OW&W had the unrivalled professional weight and expertise of Saunders, Gooch and Brunel behind them, and after a long and vicious battle in parliament the company was incorporated in 1845.

The line was to run from the GWR, just west of Oxford, to Evesham, Worcester, Droitwich, Kidderminster, Dudley and thence to Wolverhampton. It would be broad gauge throughout, with stretches of mixed gauge where it joined its narrow-gauge neighbours at Wolverhampton and Abbotswood. Thus, with provision in the enabling Act for the GWR to lease the line when finished, or to complete the works if the OW&W failed to do so, and in the meantime to appoint six out of its sixteen directors, the project was an undisguised extension of the Great Western empire. Furthermore, as principal guarantor of the new company, the involvement of the GWR was much increased by the imposition of additional works during the Bill's passage through parliament, which rendered Brunel's original estimates for the cost of the line completely inadequate. Accordingly, the GWR extended its guarantee to £2,500,000 – an arrangement which the OW&W board never formally accepted – but in promoting their fortunes on the Stock Exchange relied more on the fact of the extension than on its precise limitation. The execution of the works proceeded on the same principle, in spite of warnings from Brunel that these should be organized in such a way that some return at least should be achieved on the capital employed at the earliest possible stage. The deception could not go on indefinitely and in due course the GWR put pressure on the OW&W board and their chairman, Francis Rufford, to confront the shareholders with the facts that in its own right the company had neither money nor completed line. Captain Simmons, the Board of Trade inspector, confirmed the second point and a subsequent investigation revealed that completion would cost at least £1,500,000.

The OW&W seems to have been chastened by this exposure. Four directors resigned, including Rufford, who later went bankrupt, and in October 1850 they even managed to open four miles of line, from Abbotswood to Worcester. The new directors included Lord Ward of Dudley, who became chairman, and John Parson, who was to become a director of the Severn Valley company in 1855. For the continuation of building, tenders were accepted from Messrs Peto and Betts for the completion of the line between Oxford and Worcester, and Tipton and Wolverhampton, and from Messrs Treadwells for completion from Tipton to Worcester. Both partnerships agreed to assist in raising capital in return for some hand in the management. This arrangement, a common one in railway building, was repeated by Peto and Betts in association with Brassey on the Severn Valley line. In addition, £850,000 was to be raised by the issue of preference shares.

The enterprise thus appeared set to be completed in prosperity and concord but the healthy rivalry between the LNWR and the GWR had become cancerous over the issue of gauges and Parson was prepared to exploit it. From the time he joined the board, Parson began to invest large amounts of money in the OW&W, so large, indeed, that he was soon the largest individual shareholder. He also entered into negotiations with the LNWR and the Midland railway about the long-term future of his own company. The agreement which emerged was that the OW&W should be completed as a narrow-gauge line, partly double and partly single track, and that the LNWR and the Midland should operate it between them. Such an arrangement was a grave blow to the GWR and also of dubious legality as an application to the Court of Chancery very soon confirmed. All the GWR could do, having obtained the appropriate injunctions, was abide by the 1845 Act and prepare the terms of its own lease of the OW&W.

At a practical level, the building of the line was equally troublesome. There was even some bloodshed:

> The row was over Mickleton Tunnel and a dispute with the contractor, Marchant. It was decided to evict him, and for Peto and Betts to take over the job, which gave much trouble. So did the eviction. It was carried out on a fine June morning of 1851, by an army of navvies, numbering 2,000, from Peto and Betts and from the Great Western, under Brunel's personal command. Several fractured skulls and broken limbs resulted, but no deaths, although one character produced a gun, and was dissuaded from using it by means of a spade in lieu of a battle-axe.
>
> Hamilton Ellis, op. cit., p. 216

Such organized violence was rare, though it is true that the encampment of large gangs of navvies, most of them of foreign origin, caused nearly as much apprehension among the conservative population of rural areas as, in some respects, did the arrival of the iron monster whose path they were preparing.

Through the miasma of scurrilous business tactics, the oscillating fortunes of great companies and of individual entrepreneurs, the real impact of the coming of the railway shines. It is easy to be patroniz-

The splendid seal of the Severn Valley Railway Company
(incorporated 1853) – an enlargement of the face. The seal is
preserved in the Great Western Museum, Swindon. 'Sabrina',
prominently figuring on the seal, is the mythological goddess of the
River Severn.

O14

Severn Valley Ry
RETURN TICKET

Much Wenlock
TO
IRON BRIDGE
Second Class

Severn Valley Ry
DAY TICKET

Iron Bridge
TO
MUCH WENLOCK
Second Class
O14

SEVERN VALLEY RAILWAY

*Special ticket issued to mark five years
of the Severn Valley Railway as a voluntary organisation and the REOPENING
OF THE RAILWAY 23rd MAY 1970*

BRIDGNORTH
EARDINGTON
HAMPTON LOADE
AND RETURN

FIRST CLASS   FARE 9/-

1845

Issued subject to byelaws, regulations, conditions and notices made
by the Severn Valley Railway Company
Limited.

The fare includes one shilling donation to the Bridgnorth Bypass Rail
Bridge Trust Fund.

NOT TRANSFERABLE

Above: Severn Valley tickets.   *Left:* 1863 day return Much Wenlock
to Ironbridge.   *Right:* 1970 day return (five-year anniversary ticket
1965–70) Bridgnorth to Hampton Loade.   *Below:* Ironbridge &
Broseley station, looking towards Bewdley, 9 August 1932.

Above, left: Sir Morton Peto, 1809–89; *right:* Sir John Fowler, 1817–98,
consulting engineer to the Severn Valley Railway and builder of the
Victoria bridge at Arley. Photograph from a portrait (1868) by Sir
John Millais in the Institution of Civil Engineers.   *Below, left:*
Isambard Kingdom Brunel, 1806–59, foremost of the nineteenth-
century engineers. From an oil painting (Horsley, 1837–) in the Great
Western Museum at Swindon; *right:* Sir Daniel Gooch, 1816–89,
locomotive superintendent of the GWR. From a portrait of 1872 in
the GWR directors' board room at Paddington.

At Bridgnorth GWR station – the Clarkson steam bus, one of three such vehicles inaugurating an early road–rail link between Bridgnorth and Wolverhampton in 1904.

The Rt Hon. George Cecil Weld Forester, Member of Parliament for Wenlock 1828–74. A pioneer and director of the Severn Valley Railway Company, 1852, and Chairman, 1858–66. Photograph of the portrait in the Lady Forester Hospital at Much Wenlock, Shropshire.

Above: 'the gay nineties', a Severn Valley Railway excursion and 'booze-up' *c.* 1892. Note the gas-lit wooden carriage.   *Below:* a Sunday school outing on the Severn Valley line *c.* 1896.

Above: Neen Sollars station *c.* 1900, situated on the Bewdley to Tenbury Wells GWR line which left the Severn Valley line north of Bewdley, crossed the Severn by the Dowles bridge and proceeded via the Wyre Forest to Cleobury Mortimer, Neen Sollars, Newnham Bridge and Tenbury Wells, thence to Woofferton to join the joint GWR/LNWR main line from Hereford to Shrewsbury. *Below:* 'Sunday best at Kidderminster' *c.* 1896; note the GWR clerestory carriage and flat-topped brake at left, and goods shed on right, still in use.

Bewdley GWR station, Severn Valley branch *c.* 1910. *Above:* looking
north, showing two passenger trains headed by Dean tanks, probably
0-4-2 wheel arrangement, and *(centre)* an early steam railcar. *Below:*
looking south. A station staff of thirteen, plus station-master, extreme
right. A Bridgnorth to Kidderminster train headed by a Dean tank
engine, probably 0-4-2 wheel arrangement, stands in the station.

0-6-0 322 class no. 338 shunting at Bewdley *c.* 1925.

2-4-0 3232 class no. 3244 leaving Bewdley on a Tenbury Wells train.

455 class 0-4-0 tank no. 976 standing at Kidderminster station *c.* 1920, heading a seven-coach set of close-coupled four-wheeled wooden coaches on the Severn Valley line.

This 4-4-4 side tank (one of two) was built by Sharp Stewart of Glasgow in 1897 and rebuilt in 1925. Formerly no. 18 on the M&SWJ and no. 27 on the GWR, shown here at Bewdley c. 1925 on the Severn Valley line.

0-6-0 pannier tank no. 325 at Stourbridge Junction bound for Kidderminster and the Severn Valley line. The engine is in immaculate GWR livery, c. 1924.

Dean double-framed 0-6-0 pannier tank of the 1076 or Buffalo class, believed to be no. 1570, with a motor-train from the Severn Valley line and Bewdley, is seen entering Kidderminster c. 1925.

Buildwas station, Much Wenlock branch (high level) platform, looking towards Bewdley, 9 August 1932.

Sir Gerald Nabarro, M.P., a director of the Severn Valley Railway, on ex-GWR Collett goods, 0-6-0 no. 3205, at Bridgnorth, 19 July 1970, with driver R. J. Denson, fireman A. G. Bending and shunter D. C. Williams.

ing about the revolutionary consequences of an amenity which has
been familiar even to the grandfather of anyone now living, but the
fact is that it portended a more fundamental change in the lives of
ordinary people than any which their descendants have experienced
within the ensuing century and a half. The building of the railways,
which remains the greatest physical achievement carried out by the
human race within a comparatively short space of time, was the
supreme example of the application of the new technology, founded
on steam power and iron, of the early nineteenth century. 'Railroad
iron', wrote Emerson, 'is a magician's rod in its power to evoke the
sleeping energies of land and water.' It is true that railways were
built primarily to serve the expanding or emergent cities but in doing
so, they intruded into the most introverted parts of rural England,
'destroying', in Dr Arnold's phrase, 'feudality for ever'. The cities
were new and voracious markets not only for the produce, but for
the labour of agricultural areas. Provincial society, formerly circum-
scribed by units such as the town, estate or village, was compelled by
crude economic forces to look outwards, if not to London, then at
least to a larger and probably new local capital. By the end of the
century the population of England had become predominantly urban
and suburban in distribution and habit. It remains so on a much
enlarged scale today. The motor car has provided an alternative but
it has not yet destroyed the pattern of life and work which the railways created. It says a great deal for the vigour and self-confidence
of Victorian society that the arrival, within a very short period, of
something so utterly alien to any previous experience should, leaving
aside certain simple physical fears, have been welcomed. Perhaps
this is partially explained by the fact that almost from the start,
railways were cheaper, more reliable and at least twice as fast as
existing forms of transport, but the extent to which they were used
by people of all classes surprised even the most ambitious promoters.

Thus it was when the OW&W came to Evesham in Worcestershire
in 1852. It demanded new facilities in the ancient and placid borough
and engendered a new outlook on life among its citizens and the
inhabitants of the surrounding area. And apparently the people
welcomed it: they rang the church bells, fired ceremonial cannon and
decorated the line and station with flags and triumphal arches of
evergreens and flowers; a streamer proclaimed 'Success to the Ox.
Wor. and Wol. Railway'; and the exhortation on another banner,
'Eat, Drink, and Be Merry', was immediately fulfilled by a public
dinner in the High Street. Among the consequences of the coming of

the railway, in due course, was the provision of a hotel to serve it. In January 1868 the *Evesham Journal* reported that 'the want of accommodation for the refreshment of railway travellers connected with our railway stations at Evesham has long been felt . . . We learn that the year 1868 is in all probability destined to see this requirement fully and efficiently supplied.' The full and efficient supply of 'this requirement' was a contentious issue locally but the Railway Hotel was eventually built and licensed, though only, its first proprietor apologized, as a 'beer house'. There it stands today, opposite the station, identified by a splendid sign depicting an antique 2-2-2 type locomotive and gauntly renamed 'Railway'.

Shortly before the OW&W was opened to Evesham, Brunel had resigned as engineer. He was succeeded by John Fowler, later engineer to the Severn Valley railway, who had the unenviable job of playing out the burlesque in the matter of gauges. The OW&W, although launched as a triumph of the broad-gauge faction, was built almost entirely as a narrow-gauge railway. There had been elaborate compromises over the provision of a mixed gauge but such stretches of line appeared only on the northern sections, and even there on the down track. The company faced penalties if it failed to provide a mixed-gauge line, completed by the beginning of 1856, but Parson prevaricated and repeatedly sought extensions in the time for completion. At one stage he is reputed to have remarked: 'I want to get from Parliament three years to execute the broad gauge works . . . If I can get three years, I am of opinion that the work will never be executed at all.' The evident strategy was that, given enough delay, the GWR would lay a mixed gauge over its own line between Oxford and Reading, thus giving the OW&W access to London by way of the London & South Western and the South Eastern. The expectation was fulfilled in so far as the GWR agreed to abandon its insistence on a mixed gauge in February 1858.

The agreement was reached less than six months before work on the building of the Severn Valley line began, but from its earliest years the company seems never to have been in doubt on the question of gauge, possibly because the expectations of the promoters were always directed towards the north; most probably because of a belief in the ultimate triumph of the narrow gauge. A bigger obstacle was local indifference and this most powerful disincentive had killed all earlier schemes, including the one promoted by the Shropshire Union Railways & Canal Co. in 1846, which had gone as far as authorizing Robert Stephenson and Robert Nicholson to make some

14

preliminary surveys. With the embarrassment of the OW&W, however, and the abandonment of their early plans for a branch from
Worcester to Shrewsbury, local enthusiasm had revived. There is no
single obvious reason why. Possibly, with the developing railway
system to the east and south, it was encouraged by immediate access
to a main line, or perhaps the belated realization that only a railway
could revive the area commercially. Certainly George Griffith,
commemorating the opening of the line in 1862, thought so when he
wrote, with reference to Bewdley:

> We never thought that steam and rail,
> Would supersede the coach and sail, –
> That road and river should be shorn
> Of traffic that should ne'er return.

> And Bewdley folk cannot refrain
> From seeing the long-talk'd of train,
> O'er her proud bridge in troops they go,
> To see the entrance of her foe –
> For steam has drawn her trade away
> And brought her down to sad decay.

The board of the Severn Valley Railway Co. met for the first time
at 22 Parliament Street, Westminster, on 25 August 1852. The
chairman, Jonathan Thorp, and two other directors, Michael Graze-
brook and Major Charles Tyndale, were also directors of the OW&W;
William Reed was a director of the London & South Western and the
Rt Hon. Francis Parker, M.P., a powerful and ubiquitous figure in
railway affairs, was a director of the Great Northern. Local interests
were represented by Sir Francis Pigot, M.P. for Bridgnorth, and Col.
the Hon. George Cecil Weld Forester, M.P. for Wenlock. Pigot did
not remain with the company after its incorporation in 1853, but
Weld Forester remained on the board for nearly fifteen years and
served as chairman from 1858 to 1866. He was a very substantial and
well connected figure, nationally and locally. The Foresters are an
ancient Shropshire family, and by the time the barony was created
in 1821 they had become large landowners and the owners of extensive mineral rights. George sat in parliament for the family seat of
Wenlock for over thirty-five years from 1828 and became a Privy
Councillor and twice Comptroller of the Household. He resigned his
seat in 1874, on succeeding his brother as 3rd Baron Forester, and
died in 1886.

The first meeting of the board was concerned with working arrangements and the appointment of advisers and officers of the company. Robert Nicholson became engineer, and Messrs Toogoods, who had been involved in the 1846 project, were appointed solicitors and parliamentary agents. At two further meetings in September, bankers and brokers were appointed in London, Manchester, Liverpool and Birmingham, and Charles Reed, who held a similar post with the North & South Western Junction Railway, became secretary. The line under discussion at these early meetings was to run from Hartlebury, but only as far north as Coalbrookdale. A deputation of directors was to visit the area to explain the objects of the undertaking, test local opinion and perhaps attract investors. Accordingly, public meetings were arranged at Ironbridge, Bewdley and Bridgnorth at the beginning of October. The Bridgnorth meeting, according to the *Shrewsbury Chronicle*, was not a success:

It is not too much to say, when we state that from the apathy and neutrality evinced at this and all former meetings, the chances of a railway coming to Bridgnorth are very few.

And the *Worcester Herald* reported:

A very strong feeling was manifested that the railway would be more generally useful, as well as more acceptable, were it continued up to Shrewsbury, and the meeting declined to give the promoters a resolution to support the line until it was determined so to extend it.

The proceedings at Bewdley on Friday 8 October were more protracted. The company was represented by Jonathan Thorp and William Reed, supported by Robert Nicholson, Charles Reed and William Toogood. Among those present were the Bishop of Worcester, Sir Thomas Winnington, M.P. for Bewdley, and Pearce and William Baldwin, local businessmen. A meeting to discuss the merits of building a railway was nothing new to the people of the town. More grandiose schemes than this had withered before their icy indifference. All the old objections and doubts were wheeled out: the line would be a menace to life and property; it could never hope to compete with the river; and it would cause unemployment. There were some individuals prepared to answer the objectors with bland contradictions but none to destroy them by argument and give a positive lead in support of the promoters. However, some of the objections looked a little jaded in the circumstances of the town's decline and in any case, Thorp and his colleagues were old hands with most of the answers prepared.

Thorp blamed the failure of the earlier schemes on public inertia and the general recession in railway affairs in the late 1840s. But, he claimed, a healthier state of affairs now prevailed in the money market and it was beginning to be thought that no better sort of investment existed than in enterprises such as this one – 'investment in the high roads which have now become the only mode of communication for the community' – and in due course he hoped that many of those present would become shareholders in their own rail- way. In the meantime, he said, it was essential that they should settle all doubts and uncertainties which might prevent them from 'coming off triumphant', and in the future planning of the line the general view that it should be built as far north as Shrewsbury would receive the fullest consideration. 'It is not necessary', he continued:

for me to say one word about the numerous population of the towns and districts through which the railway is to pass, or to attempt to prove that the district deserves from its industrial wealth and importance the accommodation of the character proposed. But it has been said, 'We have a river along which the traffic of the district passes'. To this I reply, first, that the navigation is liable to interruption and impediments, and it is in the nature of the thing that a fluvial way should not always be practicable, and second, that other towns have rivers equally as serviceable, and yet the inhabitants of those towns have not for a moment hesitated to ask for additional accommodation by means of a railway, and to be thankful for it when they have got it. I should imagine there is not a man here unacquainted with the river accommodation between London and Gravesend. But the people are not satisfied even with the line now completed by the South Eastern Railway Company, which passes parallel with the river. If the river had been preferred, the line must have been almost profitless as a speculation, but there is not a more successful line anywhere. The traffic is enormous and not one passenger less goes by the river; the railway therefore has only developed traffic which would otherwise have lain dormant. An Act has actually been obtained for a railway on the opposite bank, and if we may judge of the value of a railway by the price of its shares in the market, that line is exceedingly well thought of, for its shares are considerably above par at the present moment. This shows that, however valuable river accommodation may be, the inhabitants may still expect immense advantage from the establishment of a railway.

In laying out the line care has been taken to avoid property of great value. The directors have been anxious not to interfere with that property which has been laid out for the pleasure of private individuals, and having been able to arrange a line which does little injury to valuable property they will be able to construct it cheaply, and will not give railway accommodation merely, but that accommodation at a cheap rate. In one respect this line is fortunate in not having been proceeded with in 1847, because it can now be constructed for about one fourth of the money it would then have cost. I believe I am right in saying that this line can be constructed within £10,000 per mile, such is the difference between the value of professional assistance, materials of construction, and labour, now and in 1847.

The other director present at the Bewdley meeting, William Reed, made a speech designed to assuage suspicions about the impact of the railway on agriculture and employment. He spoke, he said, with previous experience. Many years ago, as a farmer in Lincolnshire, he had ventured to propose 'Success to Railways' at an agricultural society's dinner. The toast had been received on that occasion with murmurs of dissent. Nobody would any longer doubt that railways were advantageous to agriculture but if anyone needed convincing he could not do better than repeat the argument he had used on that occasion, based on the example of the Liverpool & Manchester Railway. When the railway's Bill was before Parliament, a petition had been presented by road carriers in the area alleging that the construction of the line would produce large-scale redundancies of both men and horses who had made an average of £40,000 a year out of traffic on the highway. In addition it was claimed that without so many horses on the road, the farmers would suffer for want of a local market for their corn. Such, said Reed, were the dismal prognostications, but what had happened? Profit had gone up to as much as £100,000 a year but it certainly had not been spent on the maintenance of horses displaced from the road: it kept human beings 'men instead of four-footed animals'.

18

Back in London, at a meeting the following Wednesday, the proposal that the line should be built to Shrewsbury was accepted. Robert Nicholson was instructed to resume the planning of the line in its extended form, and the company's parliamentary agents to prepare a Bill for presentation immediately.

3
Planning

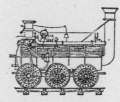

The Severn Valley Railway Co.'s first prospectus, issued in July
1852, announced that the capital of the proposed company would be
£600,000 in 30,000 £20 shares, with a deposit of two guineas per
share. 'The line', it proclaimed, 'will accommodate a country entirely
without a railway, and where the want of one is severely felt, the
whole produce of the districts being now mainly dependent for its
transit upon the navigation of the Severn, which, above Stourport, is
at all times difficult and uncertain.'

At Bewdley, Jonathan Thorp had closed the meeting with a few
words about shares. The directors, he said, were in no difficulty over
raising the necessary capital – the numerous applications for shares
'prevent any doubt upon that point; but applications for shares from
persons residing in the district will receive a preference'. There was
no rush among the potential investors in the area to avail themselves
of the preference. Local dignitaries such as Sir Thomas Winnington,
some members of the Whitmore family, Colonel Weld Forester and
his brothers Lord Forester and the Reverend Orlando, invested
about £1,000 each, and most of the directors' personal holdings were
well in excess of the qualification of fifty shares. Thorp, for example,
who was then living at Offenham, near Evesham, had £10,000 of his
own money in the project. Nicholson, the engineer, invested £5,000,
and his eventual successor, John Fowler, £1,000 at the start. Two
speculators in London, William Barry and Henry Stikeman, put in
£20,000 each. The largest individual holding was the £30,000 put up
by one of the line's builders, Thomas Brassey, though neither of his

partners – Edward Betts and Morton Peto – was among the first subscribers. The response from the local business community was disappointing. Four members of the Baldwin family – Thomas, Enoch, Pearce and William – invested only £400 between them, and organizations such as the Coalbrookdale Co. put up nothing at all until visited, at the request of the board, by Colonel Forester, and even then their participation was modest.

Though the list of applications for shares was still incomplete in November 1852, the company's general progress towards incorporation was reasonably smooth. The Oxford, Worcester & Wolverhampton Railway, which had contracted to operate the line if and when it was built, willingly amended the agreement to account for the new and longer route now proposed to Shrewsbury. Expenses were comparatively light, though the company had to support a petition against the L&NWR's Bill for a branch line to Coalbrookdale, and the engineer and solicitors asked for settlement of their accumulated expenses and that thereafter these should be rendered monthly.

The Bill was deposited for the consideration of parliament in November 1852, and the accompanying deposit of £90,000 paid into the Bank of England. By April, the list of petitioners against the Bill was complete. These included memorials from railway companies in direct or partial competition with the proposed line, such as the Shrewsbury & Chester, the Shrewsbury & Birmingham, and the Shrewsbury & Hereford. Some petitions were easily settled and never brought before the parliamentary committee on the Bill. The Shrewsbury Race Course Co., for example, only wanted one of their points of access preserved by the erection of a footbridge over the line, which was agreed to. The trustees of the Shrewsbury, Wenlock and Bridgnorth turnpike roads were bought off for £2,500, the cost of diverting a stretch of road near Cound, where the railway would have run parallel and immediately next to the existing road – the petition was based on the claim that passing trains would have terrorized alike horses and travellers by road. Robert Woodward, who had recently purchased Arley Castle, dropped his petition following an agreement that all trains on the Severn Valley line would stop at Arley at the request of himself, his children or his wife, provided that the station-master had half an hour's notice.

Thomas Charlton Whitmore was more intractable. His petition was actually heard before the committee and the evidence connected with it took up more than one day, but it was not settled there.

21

Indeed, his case was in and out of the Court of Chancery for most of the rest of the decade and the representation of the company there came to be a substantial and recurrent expense.

The Whitmores were a family of approximately the same stature in the area to the north of Bridgnorth as the Winningtons in and around Bewdley, well below the Foresters or the Clevelands but far above such emergent and predominantly commercial dynasties as the Baldwins and, even after the 1832 Reform Act, enjoyed almost proprietorial rights over the local parliamentary seats of Bridgnorth and Bewdley. The Whitmores had marked their economic and social progress by the erection of a commodious and imposing house at Apley, some 3½ miles north of Bridgnorth, set in a newly landscaped park above a bend in the river Severn. The house and estate had come into Thomas Whitmore's hands in 1846, twenty years after the new building was completed.

Jonathan Thorp had claimed at Bewdley that in planning the line the company had been anxious 'not to interfere with that property which had been laid out for the pleasure of private individuals'. In requesting the assent or dissent of owners, lessees and occupiers of land either within or close to the line of deviation fixed on the deposited plans of the railway, the company had been generally fortunate in encountering very little dissent. Whitmore was an exception. As the owner of over 5,000 acres in the area, including valuable property in Bridgnorth, he 'was exceedingly anxious to get a railway to Bridgnorth'. Indeed, he and other members of his family had been active in promoting earlier schemes to that end, at a time when he himself had represented the borough in parliament. But the present enterprise, he claimed, was misconceived and ill-designed. The line, passing within three hundred yards of his house and through his park, would 'entirely destroy the quietude and beauty of Apley'. The only settlement he would accept was the concealment of the line. Years later, Whitmore cleared some of the valuable and by then mature trees in his park in order to get a better view of the trains leaving Linley station.

The parliamentary committee on the Severn Valley Railway Bill began its sittings on Monday 9 May 1853. The members were Sir Edmund Hayes, Mr Brand, Lord Adolphus Vane, and Mr Butt, under the chairmanship of Sir James Buller East, one of the members for Winchester. They sat for nineteen days between 9 May and 27 June, and heard from ninety-seven witnesses. The cost to the company was £5,600.

The petitions from other railway companies brought before the committee represented either formal opposition or operational technicalities. Some of the former were unashamedly monopolistic in intent and inconsequential in their outcome; the latter were mostly incorporated, either wholly or by compromise, in the Act. The independent witnesses were collectively a representative cross-section of the life and commerce of the locality, a procession of opinion and prejudice from all points and professions along the proposed route.

Among those who appeared in support of the Bill was much concern about improved communications with the north, especially with ports such as Liverpool, and the expense, uncertainty and delay caused by having to transport goods and raw materials by way of Wolverhampton and the change from canal to railway there. Samuel Broom, worsted spinner, wool stapler and general merchant of Stourport, employing 120 people and importing much of his raw material from Ireland by way of Holyhead, said that the change from railway to canal at Wolverhampton caused up to ten days' delay on each shipment. Pearce Baldwin, ironfounder, employing 250 men at Stourport and consuming 1,000 tons of raw iron and 2,500 tons of coal and coke each year, spoke of similar delays and difficulties and alleged that a direct railway link with the Shropshire coalfield would enable him to obtain better and cheaper coal more quickly. In cross-examination, neither would admit that the provision of a goods station at Hartlebury, two and a half miles from Stourport, would be any solution. Nor would James Lewty, principal partner in the Wilden Iron and Tin Plate Co., when it was suggested to him that his works was almost exactly equidistant from Hartlebury and the proposed station at Stourport.

A number of witnesses were also small shareholders and some of them appeared as commercial casualties of the lack of a railway rather than as businessmen whose operations would improve with improved transport. Thomas Nock, for example, formerly an innkeeper in Bridgnorth, testified that the town had so languished for want of a railway that he had been driven out of business and into the corn trade in a small way. George Griffith, a Kidderminster corn-merchant, said that he had been compelled to move his business there from Bewdley four years before because the decline in trade, much accelerated by the arrival of the OW&W line, had made it impossible for him to continue profitably in the town of his birth.

When hostile witnesses spoke of the river as a perfectly adequate means of transport for the Severn Valley, others were produced to describe its hazards and uncertainties. Thomas Augustus Jackson, manager and agent of the Eardington and Hampton Loade ironworks, recalled that in summer 70-ton vessels could frequently take no more than 15 tons because of the lack of water.

A further aspect of the case which received considerable attention was the effect of the line on the value of property. Slade Barker, banker, magistrate and Mayor of Bewdley, not only wanted a railway in the town but was personally delighted that it was intended to pass within fifty yards of his own house. George Edmund Shuttleworth, 'disposer of gentlemen's estates', when asked whether he would attempt to play down the proximity of the railway for fear of repelling potential buyers, replied that he 'should draw the attention of the public to it as a great advantage'.

The expert witnesses were led by Nicholson, who was cross-examined for two days on engineering details, and supported by Charles Gregory, engineer of the Croydon & Epsom, Bristol & Exeter, and Somerset Central railways. Brunel appeared briefly on 1 June and was gloomy about the prospects of the line as a through route, describing the proposed termination at Shrewsbury as 'very extraordinary and very unaccountable, it seems to me to have every objection and every disadvantage.'

The first Severn Valley Railway Act, which was passed without a division early in July, received the Royal Assent on 20 August 1853. The Act was in fifty-four sections covering, as was normal, matters such as the capital of the company, defining the agreed route, and setting out rights and obligations in relation to landowners and other railway companies affected by it. The share capital was as described in the prospectus with powers to borrow on mortgage or bond up to £200,000, once the whole of the capital had been subscribed for. Section XXXIX provided that the powers of compulsory purchase under the Act should expire after three years from its passing, and section XL that the 'Railway, Branch, and Works, shall be completed within Five years of the passing of this Act', that is to say, by August 1858.

Section XIX defined the route:

1. . . . commencing by a Junction with the Main Line of the
Oxford, Worcester and Wolverhampton Railway in the Parish
of Hartlebury in the County of Worcester at or near a Point
Five and a Half Furlongs or thereabouts Southwards of the

Hartlebury Station on that Main Line, and terminating at or near a certain Road situate in the Parish of Holy Cross and St. Giles, within the Borough of Shrewsbury and the County of Salop.

2. A Branch Railway or Tramway commencing and diverging from and out of the intended Railway at or near certain Limekilns or Limeworks situate at or near Benthall Edge in the Parish of Benthall in the County of Salop, occupied by John Patten, and terminating at or near a certain Inclosure situate in the Parish of Madeley in that County.

Within two months of its incorporation, the company was looking for economies. A deviation suggested in the report of the parliamentary committee on the Bill had proposed that the new railway could join the Shrewsbury & Hereford line at Sutton Bridge junction, south of the proposed terminus, and that the two companies should share a station in Shrewsbury. Negotiations towards this end were accordingly begun, though the Shrewsbury & Hereford as uncooperative in the early stages. The issue was causing some concern by the time of the general meeting in February 1854 – one of the two general meetings between 1853 and December 1857 which did not have to be adjourned for want of a quorum. At the same meeting, Thorp announced that 'the expenditure of the Company will be confined within the narrowest possible limits'. This was, no doubt, in deference to a letter to the board from Morton Peto the previous November:

12th November, 1853.

> Somerleyton Hall,
> Suffolk.

Gentlemen,

You will feel my interest in the Severn Valley Railway as sufficient excuse for my troubling you.

I am most anxious that no expense of any kind should be incurred until we are really in a position to proceed.

You have abundance of time and if we are kept from beginning for the next three years we can then open it long before the Act required.

I need not impress on you the present state of the money market or the political condition of Europe, you know it all

perfectly well and I am confident you will see the propriety of
the course I advise.

I am, Gentlemen,

Obediently and respectfully,

S. MORTON PETO.

The 'interest' to which Peto referred was the security for £47,250
towards the parliamentary deposit of £90,000, which he and his
colleagues Brassey and Betts had put up.

Samuel Morton Peto was in many respects the model of the
Victorian entrepreneur. Enviably energetic, assiduous and successful
in a number of fields, moralistic, just and ruthless. Though he lost
much of the vast wealth he had accumulated during the financial
panic of the mid-1860s, and had to resign his seat in parliament, he
did so with honour, described by Gladstone as 'a man who has
attained a high position in this country by the exercise of rare talents
and who has adorned that position by his great virtues.' He was born
in 1809 and trained in all aspects of conventional building under his
uncle Henry. In addition to architecture, draughtsmanship and
surveying, he also acquired more earthy skills such as learning to lay
800 bricks a day. Henry Peto died in 1830 when Morton was just out
of his articles of apprenticeship, leaving the business equally between
him and another nephew, Thomas Grissell. During their fifteen years
in partnership until 1846 they were mainly concerned with general
building, working under some of the most successful architects of the
day such as the Smirke brothers and Sir Charles Barry, and executing
buildings such as the Oxford and Cambridge Club, Nelson's Column
and the Reform Club. At the time that their partnership ended they
had just won the contract for the new Houses of Parliament which
Grissell went on to build while Peto concentrated on railway construction, although they had already built much of the South
Eastern railway and all the GWR between Hanwell and Langley.

Peto immediately entered into a new partnership with Edward
Betts and their association continued until the latter's death in 1872.
Their works included the Folkestone–Hythe section of the South
Eastern, including the viaduct, tunnel and martello towers, much of
the Eastern Counties Railway, the Dorset section of the London &
South Western, and parts of the Great Northern and Great Eastern
railways. Before their interest in the Severn Valley line they had
worked in the Midlands on the Oxford & Birmingham, the OW&W,
the Hereford, Ross & Gloucester and on Sir William Cubitt's

improvements to the navigation of the River Severn. Peto and Betts, who were driven out of business in the financial panic of the mid-1860s, worked with Thomas Brassey, their colleague on the Severn Valley line, on many projects in other parts of the world, including the Grand Trunk Railway of Canada and the Victoria bridge over the St Lawrence which at the time of its opening in 1860 was by far the largest in the world. Brassey, although the contracts he took by himself were on a much more modest scale, was in and out of financial difficulty all his life. His biographer, describing him as a man almost without faults, observed that his only defect was a difficulty in saying 'No', which led to his involvement in some 'disastrous undertakings' (Arthur Helps, *The Life and Labours of Mr. Brassey*, Bell, 1872).

Betts and Brassey were single-minded engineers and contractors: Peto was a man of broader ambitions, sitting in Parliament for three different constituencies over fifteen years and serving as a commissioner for and guarantor of the Great Exhibition of 1851. In business he always tried to establish some hand in the management of the projects with which he was connected. The Severn Valley board replied to his letter of 12 November 1853 to the effect that they agreed with his views, that they did not intend to proceed with the works and that they would incur no further liability until they were in a stronger position. They made economies of a sort. Two members of the staff in the London office were dismissed, the secretary's salary was cut to £300 a year and Nicholson, who had been given an annual salary of £1,000, plus £200 expenses, was told that as the company was not for the time being going ahead with building the line, he would be paid only his professional fees in future. On the other hand, in spite of the fact that the company was under-subscribed and notwithstanding the provisions as to borrowing in the 1853 Act, they were contracting short-term loans which, in relation to the size of the company, were unhealthily large. Furthermore another Bill was in preparation, scheduled for consideration by parliament on 17 March 1854. This Bill, which was primarily intended to make changes in the course of the line and in the capital of the company of the sort that were eventually included in the 1855 Act, also included a clause continuing directors in office until the completion of the works.

The contents of the Bill were, of course, public knowledge, but Peto was apparently kept informed of the company's other activities by Major Tyndale, one of the directors, and he wrote to Thorp in April:

27

11th April 1854.

> 9, Great George Street,
> Westminster.

Dear Sir,
The statement made to me by Major Tyndale of the State of
the Company is so serious and so at variance with my
engagement with you that I have no alternative than at once
to place my interests in the hands of my Solicitors, Messrs.
Crowder and Maynard.

I also beg to give you notice I shall oppose the Bill you have
now in Parliament to make the office of directors permanent
till the works are complete and that I will call public attention
to such an attempt to deprive shareholders of the due right of
representation.

> I am, Dear Sir,
> Respectfully yours,
> S. MORTON PETO.

to which Thorp replied:

13th April 1854.

> Severn Valley
> Railway Company,
> Parliament Street,
> Westminster.

Dear Sir,
I shall be happy to give Messrs. Crowder and Maynard all the
information I possess as to the affairs of the Severn Valley
Railway Company. Not one shilling of the money of the
Company has been misapplied and I believe that every step
that has been taken has been for the benefit of the undertaking.

With reference to your remarks about the Clause continuing
the directors in office until the works are completed, I beg to
inform you that the Solicitors of the Company, Messrs. Toogood,
suggested the insertion of such a Clause, and that the Board
assented to it only on their recommendation.

> I am, Dear Sir,
> Yours respectfully,
> JONATHAN THORP

During the following fortnight Peto continued the correspondence
through his solicitors, who emphasized that their client was a very

In the early 1960s at Bewdley South box, the pioneer BR standard class 3, 2-6-2 tank no. 82000 approaches Bewdley with a four-coach set from Kidderminster.

Above: Buildwas station, Severn Valley platform, looking towards
Bewdley, 9 August 1932. *Below:* Bridgnorth to Hampton Loade
scheduled service – 1400 hrs train 19 July 1970 leaving Bridgnorth
hauled by ex-GWR Collett 0-6-0 no. 3205 with Sir Gerald Nabarro,
M.P., on the footplate.

Above: at Hartlebury, Worcestershire. Junction for the Severn Valley
line (originally a link on the OW&W line with the Severn Valley
Railway: both were absorbed into the GWR under the Act of 1872).
Here ex-GWR diesel railcar no. 26, 1208 hrs Saturdays only Hartlebury
to Bewdley, 4 July 1959, awaits departure. *Below:* at Stourport-on-
Severn, awaiting the road-crossing gates on the A451, ex-GWR
61XX, large Prairie tank no. 6118 heads the 1610 hrs Saturdays only
Hartlebury to Shrewsbury train on the Severn Valley line, 18 July
1957.

On 1 August 1960 an ex-LMS Crab 2-6-0 no. 42783 enters Bewdley station with a bank holiday excursion.

Ex-GWR 2-6-0 no. 6314 hauling coal on the Severn Valley line, seen between Northwood Halt and Bewdley on 29 May 1963. The two tracks are parallel single lines: the Bewdley–Tenbury Wells branch is in the foreground.

The Dowles bridge carrying the Bewdley–Tenbury Wells line across the River Severn. A GWR diesel railcar is on the bridge, c. 1946.

At Northwood Halt, anglers board a local train to Kidderminster headed by no. 9656 in 1961.

Above: on 29 September 1962, deputizing for a diesel railcar, ex-GWR 0-6-0 pannier tank no. 3619, shedded at Kidderminster, enters the picturesque Arley station on the Severn Valley line, hauling a southbound train comprising two ex-LMSR corridor coaches.   *Below:* the same locomotive and train, later in the day, photographed at track level.

The last scheduled passenger train operated by BR leaving Bridgnorth at 1858 hrs on Sunday 8 September 1962, double-headed by ex-GWR pannier tanks nos 9624 and 4665.

Above: Coalport, between Bridgnorth and Shrewsbury, has been the home of fine ceramics for hundreds of years. On 23 April 1957 the 1345 hrs passenger train from Shrewsbury to Kidderminster, hauled by ex-GWR no. 5518, with assorted three-coach set, stops at the station. This was the last engine of this type to work on the Severn Valley line in BR days. *Below:* on 12 July 1962 a northbound mineral train from Alveley colliery bound for Shrewsbury, passes Coalport hauled by ex-GWR 41XX class. Note the characteristic SVR station buildings.

Above: Buildwas station on the northern section of the Severn Valley line at 1650 hrs 6 June 1959. Railcar no. 29 is the 1620 hrs from Shrewsbury to Hartlebury and the ex-GWR no. 9639 enters the branch (high level) platform, on the 1640 hrs Much Wenlock to Wellington. *Centre:* at Cound Halt, 2 March 1963. Ivatt 2-6-2 BR tank no. 41240 halts with the 1730 hrs train from Shrewsbury to Bridgnorth. *Below:* at Shrewsbury on 23 August 1961 ex-GWR no. 5555 about to leave with the 1345 hrs train southbound down the Severn Valley.

Coalport station, looking towards Bewdley, 9 August 1932.

Ex-GWR Collett goods 0-6-0 no. 3205 arrives at Bridgnorth on 25 March 1967. Note the GWR coat of arms on the headboard and Telford church right background.

Above: 'contemporary steam' on Oldbury viaduct, Bridgnorth, 23 April 1967, ex-LMSR Ivatt 2-6-0 no. 46443 and ex-GWR Collett 0-6-0 no. 3205.

Opposite: 'gardeners' delight' – the condition of the line between Hampton Loade and Alveley in 1967.

On Sunday 31 March 1968 no. 3205 nearing the Victoria bridge, Arley.

On Sunday 24 May 1970, no. 3205 on the 1600 hrs train from Bridgnorth to Hampton Loade at Knowle Sands.

large shareholder who, unlike most of the others, was more or less fully paid up and that his prestige in such matters as the construction of railways would ensure that his opposition to the Bill would not go unheard. As a result, on 3 May, Peto was elected a director and on 8 May the Bill was withdrawn. Ten days later Jonathan Thorp and Francis Parker resigned, to be replaced by William Jackson, another M.P., and Peto became chairman.

Peto held the chair for a little over three years. Though for a year after his resignation none of his colleagues was willing to take his place and even though the deputy chairman, John Parson, talked mainly in terms of abandoning the project during the interregnum, Peto was himself convinced at the time of his departure that the completion of the line was assured and that he could safely revert to his role as contractor. There were minor administrative changes under his leadership such as the move to share an office and thus half the rent and expenses with the Wimbledon & Croydon Railway, but the substance of Peto's contribution to the company was the planning and content of the Severn Valley Railway Acts of 1855 and 1856.

The 1855 Act, which received the Royal Assent on 30 July that year, although, with 102 sections, nearly twice the length of the 1853 Act, was uncontroversial even by the standards of its predecessor, and evidence before the parliamentary committee filled only one slender volume. The reason was that Peto had resolved most of the difficulties by prior negotiation, particularly in connection with the proposed running rights over the Shrewsbury & Hereford Railway into Shrewsbury from Sutton Bridge Junction. Relations between the two companies were good and section LXXVII of the Act left the potentially abrasive issue of the precise terms of the running rights to them.

The Act had two principal objectives: to cut the cost of construction by deviations in the proposed route, and to fix the capital at a more realistic level. The economies in construction were achieved in three ways. First, by leaving the OW&W main line north instead of south of Hartlebury; second, by crossing the Severn once only, at Arley, and then keeping to the west bank saving, according to the first estimates, £8,000 on a bridge at Quatford and £9,000 on what would have been a third crossing of the river at Bridgnorth; and third, by avoiding yet another bridge at Shrewsbury, estimated to cost £10,000, and sharing the last mile of line with the Shrewsbury & Hereford. The capital was reduced to £480,000 – the amount subscribed at the time of the company's incorporation two years before – in 24,000 £20 shares, and borrowing powers reduced proportionately to £160,000.

In June the following year a deputation of directors visited Stourport, Ironbridge, Bewdley and Bridgnorth with the by now familiar purpose of attracting further local investment. Over the previous ten years the inhabitants of the area had been told no less than five times that a railway would transform their way of life. Indeed, they had heard it all before from representatives of this very Company and so it was hardly surprising that they were indifferent.

The Severn Valley Railway Act of 1856, passed the following month, was described in the preamble as an 'Act for facilitating the Completion of their Undertaking', and section XXII gave shareholders the option of converting shares into half shares. This was two years before the date originally set for the completion of the line and clearly the time was fast approaching when work would have to begin if there was to be any chance whatever of being open on time. However, there were some encouraging developments. The terms of the OW&W's lease on the railway were agreed and in July 1857, Messrs Smith and Knight, contracting engineers, came forward and offered to prepare estimates for the work. Peto, having started the process of getting yet another Severn Valley Railway Act (passed in 1858), principally to extend the time for the completion of the works until July 1861, wrote to the board informing them of his confidence that work would soon begin.

28th July 1857.

9, Great George Street,
Westminster.

Gentlemen,
As it is now necessary that arrangements should be made for the construction of your line, it is essential that I should rightly understand the position in which I am placed with the Company.

It will, no doubt, be in your recollection that when this understanding was first established I and my friends agreed to take shares to the amount of £225,000 upon the understanding that my firm were to be contractors for the works at prices to be arranged with the Company's engineer. At a subsequent period it was unfortunately discovered that the Company's finances were in a very unsatisfactory state owing to a variety

30

of names having been put down in the list of subscribers who were not competent to fulfil their engagements.

At this crisis, I entered into the direction and was placed in the chair of the Company with a view to set matters to rights and I am happy to think that since that period, the exertions of myself and my colleagues have been attended with beneficial results.

My continuance in the direction would, of course be inconsistent with my being interested in the contract and I think it therefore right to inform you that I am prepared to retain the interests in the Company for which I have subscribed and to take the contract for the works, as originally intended, provided the Company feel themselves in a position to provide the additional funds requisite for carrying out the undertaking.

With a view, therefore, to their entering upon this question, I think it right now to retire from the direction, and beg you will consider this letter as an intimation of my resignation.

Whenever the directors are prepared to enter upon the subject I shall be ready to agree to the terms of a contract for the construction of the works, upon being satisfied that the necessary funds will be forthcoming on the part of the Company.

I am, Gentlemen,

Your very obedient servant,

S. MORTON PETO.

Without Peto, the affairs of the company soon began to go downhill again. John Parson and George Forester shared the duties of chairman until Forester was prevailed upon to take them over permanently in February 1858, but before that, faced with the prospect of raising another £85,000, a special general meeting on 29 December authorized the directors to apply for a Bill of abandonment.

4
Building

The special general meeting in December 1857 which authorized the directors to apply for a Bill of abandonment also gave them authority to proceed with the Bill for an extension of time for the completion of the works. Forester announced at the next general meeting on 26 February 1858 that 'until a very recent period the directors saw no possibility of completing the undertaking' but they had been encouraged to delay any irrevocable action towards winding up the undertaking by Sir Morton Peto and his colleagues who, 'in view of their very large stake in the railway wished to look further at the possibility of completion'. Their tender for the work, and the suggestion that part-payment to the extent of £240,000 in shares at par would be acceptable, was presented to the board at the beginning of February. This development undoubtedly saved the scheme from disaster, indeed, Forester was so confident at the February general meeting that he announced that work could begin within two months and be finished by the end of 1859.

The tender submitted by Brassey, Peto and Betts was to complete the whole line, excluding surveying, preliminary engineering and legal costs, and stations, if they amounted to more than £22,500, for £469,740 if a double track was laid throughout. Alternatively, they estimated that a single line throughout could be completed for £363,690, and a single line with works wide and substantial enough to take a second track in due course, at £389,690. Initially, the board was inclined to go for the cheapest possible and make a single track railway only. Such, at any rate, were the terms in which Forester spoke at the general meeting in February. The total cost of the line, he said, would be £530,000, or £13,000 a mile, which was well above the original estimate of 'within £10,000 per mile'. The total was made up of the contractors' lowest estimate of £363,000 and £170,000 for land and all other expenses. With the contractors to be paid £240,000 in shares, and with the borrowing powers of £160,000 under the 1855 and 1856 Acts, this proposal, said Forester, left the company with £130,000 to find, a burden that was largely borne by Thomas Brassey personally.

The line as built was on the larger model, with room for a second line to be added over most of it. The reversal of policy was largely due to the influence of John Fowler, who had favoured the more substantial plan throughout and described the additional expense as 'desirable and modest'. Fowler had succeeded Robert Nicholson as engineer to the line in 1855 but had been comparatively inactive because of the general moribundity of the scheme during the intervening years. In the period of very nearly three years between his appointment and the beginning of work in the late summer of 1858, he was paid less than £2,000 in professional fees, although this is partly accounted for by the fact that he took over much of Nicholson's preliminary work, and is certainly no reflection of the influence which he exercised over the later development of the scheme.

John Fowler was a character quite unlike Morton Peto. At no time did he have a large financial stake in the company, nor did he attempt to have any direct influence over its management. However, he was one of the greatest practical engineers of the second half of the nineteenth century and was held in particularly high regard by his professional colleagues. His training had been practical and he was fortunate in so far as one of his masters was John Rastrick, with whom he worked on the London & Brighton line, but he always lamented that his knowledge had not been more scientifically based from the start. By the time the Severn Valley line was opened in 1862, he was forty-five, and his greatest achievements were still to come, although he had had a highly successful practice in London since 1844, participating to the full in the railway mania as a much-called expert witness before parliamentary committees on railway Bills.

Somewhat surprisingly, Fowler is probably best known as the engineer of the Metropolitan Line in London – he is shown with a plan of it in the portrait reproduced in this book – but his greatest works were undoubtedly his bridges. The Victoria bridge over the

Severn at Arley, completed in 1861, and its near-identical twin at
Buildwas, the Albert Edward bridge, just off the Severn Valley line
proper, had been preceded the year before by Fowler's Pimlico
bridge, the first railway bridge over the Thames in London. Both, of
course, were far surpassed by the great cantilever structure over the
Forth in the 1880s, on which Fowler collaborated with Sir Benjamin
Baker, a former pupil, Thomas Harrison and W. H. Barlow. At the
age of sixty-three he tried to enter parliament, as a Conservative at
Tewkesbury, but was defeated and five years later, in 1885, withdrew
from another campaign in Hallamshire before polling day. He died in
1898, at the age of eighty-one.

Brassey, Peto and Betts's tender was prepared in close consulta-
tion with Fowler, and the ensuing works were to be under the
constant surveillance either of the chief engineer or his assistant, the
resident engineer, Henry Orlando Bridgman. The contract for building the railway was completed between the company and the contracting engineers on 26 May 1858. The contractors were to maintain
bridges, stations, tunnels and other works for twelve months after
the opening of the line to traffic; they were to find labour, to provide
competent superintendents and to prosecute the works continuously;
to compensate parties for damage, not to injure roads and to
indemnify the company in respect of damages and claims arising
from breaches of the contract.

The gang of navvies used for the building was drawn for the most
part from the remnants of those who had built the OW&W and the
Worcester & Hereford Railway, though Bridgman had to make a
special visit to Liverpool in May 1859 in order to enlarge the labour
force. When at full strength – only about 900, at most – the work
gangs must have been an intimidating presence in the area, but the
progress of building seems to have been entirely peaceful from this
point of view and no action was ever necessary over the section in the
contractors' agreement which read:

> The Contractors will take all requisite precautions and use their
> best endeavours to prevent any riotous or unlawful behaviour
> among their workmen, and others employed on the said works,
> and for the preservation of the peace and protection of the
> inhabitants and the security of the property in the
> neighbourhood of the said works.

Included in the contractor's agreement were some details of the
specification to which the line was to be built. Great care was to be

taken over fencing, generally made by posts and rails or posts and wire, though Apley Park was to be protected by iron hurdle fencing. Earthworks – cuttings and embankments – were to be formed to a width of 30 feet at formation level unless the engineer directed otherwise, and all slopes were to be 'soiled to six inches in depth and planted with grass seed at the appropriate season'. No rail on the line was to be less than 24 feet long, nor weigh less than 70 lb per yard and each to rest upon not less than seven sleepers, 8 feet 6 inches long and $9 \times 4\frac{1}{2}$ inches in section. The use of transverse sleepers throughout attracted some interest locally and the correspondent of the *Worcester Herald*, reporting on the progress of the building, dwelt on them at length, regarding them as preferable to 'longitudinal baulks and flat-bottomed rails used on the West Midland and other lines, the former being considered not only as presenting a greater resistance to heavy bodies in motion, but were also more economical.' Ballast was to be laid at 5 cubic yards per lineal yard and could be mixed with broken stone at the bottom, but the upper portion and boxing were to be gravel, 'the best and cleanest that can be procured in the district'. Tunnels were to be 24 feet wide and 16 feet high, and at Bridgnorth the contractors were to be responsible for any damage caused to houses in the town.

One way and another, it was a harrowing period for the local population. At Bridgnorth, the burrowing and tunnelling of the contractors in the bowels of the borough caused grave disquiet, and dwellers in the vicinity of Wribbenhall viaduct at Bewdley had to endure, as work progressed, the sudden visitations of the contractors' trains coming upon them as if from the sky.

In February Forester had hoped that work would begin in the spring of 1858. At the general meeting in August, with John Parson in the chair, it was reported that work had been delayed until the Act allowing more time for completion had been passed, and that this had now been granted. Work in fact began on 14 August and John Fowler was able to report that

> the works on some of the heaviest portions of the line are now in progress.
>
> The Contractors have been put into possession of land for a length of nearly two and a half miles at Stourport, Highley, Chelmarsh, Bridgnorth and Broseley, and are prosecuting the works with energy; and having sent materials to Ironbridge, Bridgnorth, Arley, Bewdley and Stourport, they are prepared to

enter on any portion of the line as soon as the arrangements for the purchase of the land are in a sufficiently forward state.

The viaduct across the valley of the Stour will be commenced immediately and several other large bridges; and the cutting through the sandstone rock at the entrance to the tunnel under the town of Bridgnorth is begun.

The ground over which the line was to run was generally difficult but, apart from the river itself, presented no outstanding obstacles. The major hazard turned out to be earth slips, principally caused by the exceptionally wet weather during the summer of 1860. There were two short tunnels, both through soft sandstone, at Bridgnorth and Mount Pleasant, about a mile and a half south of Bewdley. The building of the Mount Pleasant tunnel was the occasion of one of the very few fatal accidents to have occurred on the line either in building or operation. In this case, during blasting in January 1861, one of the gang named Jessie Bishop was caught in a shower of falling rock and killed almost immediately.

In February 1869 Parson told the general meeting that 'the position of the Company improves'. There was, however, some difficulty over shares and the directors had been obliged to forfeit a large number on which 'the deposit and calls are irrecoverable'. Fowler reported that

the acquisition of land for the purposes of the most important works on the line has been steadily attended to and the Contractors have placed men and materials on the ground as soon as they have had permission to do so. At the present time seven of the cuttings on the line have been completed and fourteen more are in progress.

Ten of the bridges are also in progress, including the viaduct across the Stour at Stourport. A considerable number of rails and permanent way materials have been delivered.

The quantity of land actually in the hands of the Contractors at the present time is eleven miles and sixty chains but I am informed that a large additional quantity will be ready in a very short time.

I see no reason to doubt that the line may be opened throughout on 1st October, 1860.

Fowler's estimate of the completion date was always over-optimistic but throughout his early reports he emphasized that their feasibility was wholly dependent on the availability of land. Indeed, the lack of land for the contractors to work on became quite an issue between them and the management of the company. Parson, however, stoutly maintained that the supply of land was fully up to what the contractors could usefully work and by the time of the next general meeting in August 1859, he announced that they had been able to give them possession of 'lands equal to their demands'. Fowler reported:

> Considerable difficulty has been experienced in several places on the line, from the slippery nature of the ground; and at one point, especially, between Bewdley and Bridgnorth, it has been found necessary to make a deviation from the original direction of the railway to an extent which involves considerable alteration in the character of the works to be executed.

It should still be possible, however, to finish by the end of the following year. A very large earth slip just north of Highley later in the year necessitated another deviation in order to take the line round it.

On 24 November 1859 the foundation stone of the Victoria bridge at Arley was laid. The ceremony was performed by Bridgman to an accompaniment of cheers and firing cannon. In his speech he congratulated all concerned in the building of the line so far and called for three cheers for the success of the Severn Valley Railway and the Severn bridge. A paper was placed under the foundation stone, signed by the principal gentlemen present, which read:

> The foundation stone of this bridge was laid by Henry Orlando Bridgman, Esq., C.E., Resident Engineer, on the 24th day of November, in the year of Our Lord one thousand, eight hundred and fifty-nine, and in the twenty-third year of the reign of Her Majesty, Queen Victoria. The arch of the bridge is to be constructed principally of cast-iron – 200 feet span – and, up to the present time, will be the largest cast-iron arch constructed in these kingdoms. John Fowler, Esq., Engineer-in-Chief, London; Messrs. Brassey, Peto and Betts, Contractors, also of London. The railway works were commenced in the autumn of 1858, and are expected to be completed and the line opened to the public in the spring of 1861. This railway commences at Shrewsbury, and terminates at the Hartlebury station of the Oxford, Worcester and Wolverhampton Railway, a distance of 40 miles.

Work on the bridge progressed smoothly throughout. In the following February, Fowler reported that 'the foundations are well advanced and the Coalbrookdale Company have been entrusted by Messrs. Brassey, Peto and Betts, with the execution of the castings and wrought ironwork for the superstructure.' Elsewhere the contractors were in possession of 'upwards of 34½ miles of line, and nine miles already prepared for permanent way'. Plans for stations were also ready and work on them about to begin. These were all built by Messrs Eassie & Sons of Gloucester, in brick made by Messrs Matthews & Co. of Stourbridge, who also supplied other sorts of brick for the bridges, tunnels and in some of the cuttings.

During 1860 the works were particularly afflicted by slips, including some sections which were supposedly finished. Nevertheless, they were 'progressing satisfactorily and with as much expedition as is compatible with permanently safe and substantial work.' During the year, they began 'to assume a more finished appearance', with 21 miles of line ballasted and laid, and the erection of the arch of the Victoria bridge begun.

The line was in fact complete and ready throughout to receive traffic in the autumn of 1861, but because of previous difficulties and particularly the succession of slips, Fowler advised that to 'obtain a permanently substantial formation for the permanent way, time for consolidation is essential.' Accordingly, the opening was delayed for another six months.

Table I. MILEAGES

	From Hartlebury		*From Kidderminster*	
	Mls	*Chs*	*Mls*	*Chs*
Hartlebury	0	00		
Hartlebury Junction	0	27		
Leapgate siding	1	65		
Stourport Sand siding	2	12		
Stourport-on-Severn	2	66		
Burlish Halt & siding	3	31		
Mount Pleasant tunnel (123 yd)	{4	16		
	4	21½		
Kidderminster			0	00
Kidderminster Junction			0	28
Whitehouses's Sand siding			0	70
Foley Park Halt			1	42
Bewdley tunnel (480 yd)			{1	78¾
			2	20½
Rifle Range Halt			2	71
Bewdley Junction S. box	5	24½	3	31½
Bewdley	5	40	3	47
Bewdley Junction N. box	5	44½	3	51½
Northwood Halt	7	09	5	16
Folly Point siding (site)	7	48	5	55
Victoria bridge	8	47	6	54
Arley	9	06	7	13
Kinlet siding	10	27	8	34
Highley	11	33	9	40
Alveley Halt	11	73	10	00
Alveley colliery siding	12	20½	10	27½
Hampton Loade	13	45	11	52
Eardington	15	71	13	78
Knowle Sands Brickworks siding				
Bridgnorth	18	05¾	16	12¾
Bridgnorth tunnel (550 yd)	{18	24¾	16	31¾
	18	49¾	16	56¾
Linley	22	36	20	43
Coalport	25	00	23	07
Jackfield Halt (new position)	25	49	23	56
Maw & Co.'s siding (private)	25	56	23	63
Jackfield Halt (original position)	25	67	23	74
Jackfield siding	26	35	24	42
Ironbridge & Broseley	27	00	25	07
Buildwas Junction	28	13	26	20
Buildwas Station	28	35½	26	42½
Buildwas Power Station siding	28	42½	26	49½
Buildwas Sand siding	28	69½	26	76½
Cressage	32	24	30	31
Cound Halt	33	55	31	62
Berrington	36	24	34	31
Burnt Mill Junction	39	53	37	60
Sutton Bridge Junction	39	71	37	78
Shrewsbury Station	40	52¾	38	59¾

5
Opening

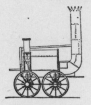

Section XL of the Severn Valley Railway Act of 1853 had required the line and associated works to be completed by August 1858, and the extension granted by the 1856 Act amounted to less than one extra year. As we have seen in the previous chapter, the company had to apply for a further extension of three years – to July 1861 – in order to make sure of fulfilling their commitment.

Long before the work was begun, however, the directors had the ultimate disposal and operation of the line in hand. Negotiations with the Oxford, Worcester & Wolverhampton Railway for this and other purposes had been going on almost continually since the time of the incorporation of the company in August 1853. These protracted discussions led to the survey of the line and its prospects by Messrs Watkin and Sherriff, who submitted their report to the board of the OW&W, in July 1857. Edward Watkin had previously been general manager of the Manchester, Sheffield & Lincolnshire Railway and had joined the board of the OW&W with Sir Morton Peto, at the time of the resignation of John Parson as its chairman in June 1856. A. C. Sherriff also joined the OW&W after the upheaval of 1856 as general manager, a post which he continued to hold under the West Midland Railway Co. His former position was traffic manager of the North Eastern Railway. As a result of their report, the OW&W agreed to take a lease of 999 years on the line. The consequences for the Severn Valley Railway were immediate. Sir Morton Peto exchanged his role as chairman for that of contractor, and the security which the OW&W lease portended finally removed any possibility that the project should be abandoned altogether, although the precise arrangements were superseded by events.

As a comparatively late starter, the Severn Valley Railway was unusually vulnerable to encroachments by larger companies. In this respect it could be said that the position of the OW&W as its adopted parent was unfortunate. Not only was the OW&W financially insecure itself at this time; quite apart from its scandalous operational history, it was regarded as already practically leased to the GWR on account of the powers to lease or sell to the latter in the Act of incorporation and the agreements between the two companies reached in August and September 1844. Now, in the late 1850s, one of the orgies of acquisition and amalgamation which characterized all British railway history from time to time was in full spate. For a small company such as the Severn Valley, the threat was a double one. Not only did it face the prospect of needless and debilitating operational rivalry but it also naturally had to go through the formality of petitioning against competing schemes as they appeared before parliament. Thus in January 1857 the L&NWR had deposited a Bill for the construction of a railway to Coalport from the Shropshire Union Railway at Hadley, and so the Severn Valley Co., which had already spent vast sums on litigation and on representation before parliamentary committees, incurred yet more expense.

Not all amalgamations were unwelcome, nor were the circumstances surrounding them invariably acrimonious. The formation of the West Midland Railway, of which the Severn Valley line became a part, was a happy undertaking. A line between Worcester and Hereford, joining the existing lines of the OW&W and the Newport, Abergavenny & Hereford Railway, had been planned for many years and a company had even been incorporated to construct it in 1853. But the project failed through lack of financial support and the proposal lay in abeyance for four years until the Newport, Abergavenny & Hereford Co. persuaded the OW&W to join them in reviving it. The necessary Act was passed in 1858 and the line opened as far as Malvern Link in July of the following year and completed to Hereford two years later. The collaboration led to proposals for permanent amalgamation of the three companies – the OW&W, the Newport, Abergavenny & Hereford and the Worcester & Hereford. An Act which came into force on 1 July 1860, brought about the union under the name 'West Midland Railway'.

At the time of its formation the West Midland Railway consisted of about 173 miles of line: from Oxford to Bushbury junction,

Wolverhampton, with branches to Chipping Norton, Stratford-on-Avon, to the Midland Railway at Abbotswood and Stoke Prior, to Malvern Wells, and to the London & North Western at Tipton; and from Hereford to Pontypool and Newport. To complete the network the company was actively interested in acquiring a further 70 miles of line from various enterprises either authorized or in course of construction, including the 15 miles from Bewdley to Tenbury, the $3\frac{1}{2}$ miles from Buildwas to Much Wenlock, and the 40 miles along the Severn Valley between Hartlebury and Shrewsbury.

Under the West Midland Railway Act, the OW&W was the constituent company and the Newport, Abergavenny & Hereford and the Worcester & Hereford companies were dissolved and merged with it under the new title. Thus the working agreement already signed between the OW&W and the Severn Valley Co. was taken over as it stood and reincarnated in the form of the Severn Valley Railway Leasing Act which came into force on 1 November 1860. Large profits were expected, and so the 55 per cent of gross traffic receipts which the West Midland was to receive on its 999-year lease was regarded as very satisfactory. In addition, the Act gave the West Midland powers to purchase the line if this was considered desirable or necessary. A special general meeting of the Severn Valley Co. was held on 31 October 1860 to approve the terms of the lease, and a complementary meeting of the West Midland took place at Worcester the following day.

At the half-yearly meeting of the Severn Valley Co. in the previous July, the possibility of opening the line to traffic between Hartlebury and Bewdley that same autumn had been suggested. At the time, the whole line was expected to be ready for opening within about a year and consequently the proposal for partial opening was rejected. Nevertheless, the line was naturally used by the contractors as and when stretches of it became available. The extent to which this was possible was inevitably inhibited by the fact that the northern half of the line was not accessible from the south until after the completion of the Victoria bridge in May 1861, and was disrupted thereafter by earth slips between Arley and Bridgnorth.

The inhabitants of the area, and in particular the citizens of Bridgnorth and Shrewsbury, were able to travel on various railway excursions before the official opening, notably to the sporting and artistic festival known as the 'Olympic Games', held at Much Wenlock at Whitsun 1861.

And so, at last, in the twilight of the railway mania, the opening approached. It is sobering to reflect at this point that no less than sixteen years divided the idea and the achievement of a line over the 50 or so miles between Worcester and Shrewsbury; and that between the first board meeting presided over by Jonathan Thorp in Parliament Street, Westminster, on 25 August 1852 and the inaugural run on 31 January 1862 nearly a decade had elapsed. The enterprise had required three Acts of parliament and much litigation; the original company had been absorbed; and a major competitor – the Great Western's line from Wolverhampton to Shrewsbury – had been opened. But the whole area was intoxicated at the prospect of commercial rejuvenation.

Colonel Yolland, the Board of Trade inspector, had been over the line on 20 January and approved the grant of the certificate for the railway to begin operations on Saturday 1 February. West Midland Railway timetables published in local newspapers duly appeared with an additional panel headed 'Severn Valley Branch'. The grant of the certificate was not altogether a formality. Throughout planning and building – perhaps because of the difficult nature of the terrain – curves, gradients and, above all, the siting and maintenance of level crossings had been subject to unusually close official surveillance, and even at the time of Colonel Yolland's inspection there was still some doubt about a minor crossing between Hartlebury and Stourport.

The opening was preceded by much consideration of the march of progress, evidenced, for example, by a comparison of the eighteenth-century bridge at Ironbridge and Sir John Fowler's masterpiece at Arley, as a correspondent of *Eddowes Salopian Journal* observed on 29 January.

The line will open at a season of the year when the valley will scarcely appear to advantage to the tourist. Nevertheless, the advantage and convenience of the route will be the same, and there are features which even now, cannot fail to attract an interested traveller.

Among them are those well known triumphs of engineering skill at Arley and Ironbridge, both of which are fine examples of the adaptation of iron to purposes to which it has been applied. One is just double the span of the other, the progress of engineering science having enabled the company which triumphed over the first difficulties so far as to surpass what was generally regarded at the time as a first experiment. The

43

Iron Bridge, which gave its name to the town it called into existence was, it is well known, designed by a Shrewsbury architect and executed by the Coalbrookdale Company, and although some little error in judgement was committed in making the arch to depend upon the equilibrium for its stability, whereby some trifling flaw occurred in the arch – more probably, after all, from some defect in the abutments, which were forced inwards by the pressure of earth – yet it still stands, a noble achievement for the time at which it was erected.

The new Bridge at Arley is just twice its span, the former being, in round numbers, 100 feet across, and the latter 200 feet. Both form pleasing features of the valley, from their noble span, their altitude, their lightness, and general aspect. They show how admirably, too, a combination of cast and wrought metal may be made serviceable for such purposes. Costly as this bridge has been, it is cheaper and more effective than one of stone, and much more light and airy than one of cast iron could have been, for while the former will bear but a force of five tons to the square inch, cast iron will bear forty, and whilst the latter will resist extension at the rate of three to seven tons only to the square inch, good wrought iron, from its stringy and fibrous character, will resist seventeen or eighteen tons. As we have said, it is twice the span of the iron bridge across the Severn higher up, and is the largest cast iron arch in the kingdom; and there are land arches of thirty feet span on each side, which give relief and effect to the solid masonry. The long arch consists of four ribs, each cast in segments of seven tons each, and tested at a pressure of seventy-five tons, whilst the joints, by being made perfectly true, add much to the strength of the work. The spandrills are fixed perpendicularly on the outer edge of the ribs (which are four feet deep and two feet thick) and firmly bound together by wrought iron bracings. On the top of the spandrills are balks, which carry the rails. Girders are fixed on the spandrills to divide or regulate the weight, so that each spandrill shall bear an equal share. The total weight of the bridge is, we believe, about five hundred tons.

The opening had originally been fixed for Saturday 1 February but as that date clashed with market day in Bridgnorth it was abandoned in favour of Friday 31 January. It was a major provincial event. Winningtons, Whitmores, Foresters and Baldwins, landowners,

Rebirth of the Severn Valley Railway. At Bridgnorth on 23 May 1970 no. 3205 heads an ex-GWR train from Bridgnorth to Hampton Loade. Awaiting departure is the 1500 hrs, hauled by no. 46443.

Above: 'Preservationists' delight' – on 22 April 1967 ex-LMSR Ivatt 2-6-0 no. 46443, property of Richard Willcox, Esq., of Stroud, Glos., at Knowle Sands on her day of arrival on the Severn Valley line (all weeds since removed). *Below:* Bridgnorth Steam Gala on 15 October 1967: no. 46443 admired by hundreds of steam engine fans.

Opposite: Co-operation with British Rail on Sunday 25 October 1970. Z15, a six-coach 'special' hauled by no. 3205, leaving Bridgnorth.

Above: on Saturday 21 March 1970 no. 46443 leaves Hampton Loade
with a rake of three ex-GWR coaches bound for Bridgnorth.

Opposite: spring in the Severn Valley. At Hay bridge, Eardington,
24 May 1970, the second day of scheduled services on the reopened
Severn Valley line, no. 46443 worked the 1735 hrs train from Hampton
Loade to Bridgnorth.

'Britannia', ex-BR 4-6-2 Pacific class no. 70000 now operates with pride and splendour on the Severn Valley line.

Above: ex-LMSR Ivatt Class 4 2-6-0 no. 43106, arrives on the Severn Valley line on 2 August 1968; here seen passing Hampton Loade northbound to Bridgnorth. *Below:* on 24 May 1970 no. 43106 leaves Bridgnorth with the 1300 hrs train for Hampton Loade.

Above: 'steam to spare', and an immaculate permanent way: no. 43106 working an afternoon train to Hampton Loade, May 1970.

Opposite: 'full steam ahead' – no. 43106 at Oldbury Grange in 1970 on 1200 hrs train from Bridgnorth to Hampton Loade, manned by driver J. Beaman and fireman D. Shadwell.

Ex-GWR diesel railcar no. 22, owned by Western Preservations Ltd (now operating on the Severn Valley line), working a Saturday shoppers' service.

Severn Valley locomotives at Bolton, Lancs, running sheds: Stanier class 8F 2-8-0 no. 48773 (now restored to the original LMS no. 8233) and class 5, 4-6-0 no. 45110.

Above: no. 8233 crossing Fowler's Victoria bridge at Arley, 16 May 1970.

Opposite: no. 8233 (now owned by the Stanier 8F Locomotive Society). *Above:* leaving Bridgnorth on the 1800 hrs train for Hampton Loade on Sunday 24 May 1970. Note the 'Night Scot' headboard. *Centre:* near Eardington with a five-coach train, the same day. *Below:* at Oldbury Grange heading the 1700 hrs train from Bridgnorth to Hampton Loade on 19 July 1970.

'Under starter's orders' at Bridgnorth, 29 March 1970.

Ex-GWR tank no. 4566, owned by the 45XX Preservation Society, being restored at Bewdley ready for service on the Severn Valley line in 1972.

'R.A.F. Biggin Hill', Stanier class 5 no. 45110. *Above:* double-heads no. 44949 on a Severn Valley Society and Manchester Rail Travel Society 'special' on 20 April 1968. Photographed at Whaley Bridge on the Stockport–Buxton line. *Below:* on the Severn Valley line, 20 September 1970.

ironmasters and humbler tradesmen alike, joined in uninhibited celebration of the evidence of progress among them, even though the early registers of shareholders in the company indicate that Victorian lucre had warmed more readily at the original prospect than had Norman blood.

The first official train left Shrub Hill station in Worcester at a little after half past eleven with nearly a hundred people aboard, including Lord Shelburne, chairman of the GWR, Mr John Fowler, Sir Thomas Winnington, M.P. for Bewdley, the Rt Hon. George Cecil Weld Forester, M.P. for Wenlock and chairman of the Severn Valley Railway Co. since 1858 and Mr A. C. Sherriff, manager of the West Midland Railway. The train was to call at all the stations, picking up further parties of dignitaries with appropriate ceremony at each of them.

The River Severn was swollen with winter rain and in more than one place had burst its banks. Nevertheless, the charm and beauty of the country through which the line passed attracted much comment and confirmed the expectation that it would be an environmental as well as a commercial amenity.

By the time the train reached Bridgnorth, the twenty-two carriages were nearly full. However, the town being roughly half-way along the company's line naturally required some special ceremony and so the band of the Bridgnorth Rifles, who had accompanied the train throughout, alighted outside the station in order to play the train in to the strains of 'See the Conquering Hero Comes!', a tune much associated with steam engines from the days of the 'Rocket' onwards. The party left Bridgnorth fortified by champagne and sherry at the expense of the Mayor, Mr W. Jones, and the train proceeded to Shrewsbury, arriving a little before two o'clock, passing Apley Park (still, at that date, unseen from Mr Whitmore's drawing-room) and cheering crowds in all the more populous districts.

The civic banquet that evening in Bridgnorth was attended by all who had bought return tickets for the inaugural run, as well as by dignitaries of the county and town, while employees of the contractors and the railway company were generously entertained elsewhere. The rival borough of Bewdley gave a similar public dinner at the George Hotel on the following Tuesday, 4 February. This event, it was said, was 'literally packed; in fact it was so crowded that it was a difficult task for the waiters to perform their functions'. There, between glees such as 'King Canute' and 'When Stormy Winds Do

Blow', Sir Thomas Winnington spoke of 'the quickening influence of
the new power placed within their reach'.

It was not, he said, his intention to detain them at any length in
going through the chequered existence of the railway during the years
since it was ushered into life by the parliamentary committee. He
well remembered the struggle it underwent at that time and how its
intrinsic merits carried the way before it when it was strongly
opposed by the landed proprietors, or at least a great portion of them,
on the line. Perhaps the most important opposition at one time had
been that of the Great Western Railway but, he was happy to say,
the powerful aid which was given to their opponents at that time
was in future to be exerted in their favour. (Cheers) The whole of the
aristocracy of Shropshire, with the exception of his gallant friend
Colonel Forester, were banded together to oppose the Bill as it
passed the ordeal it had to encounter, but still it succeeded. He
believed that the agricultural interest of the neighbourhood would
prosper by the formation of the railway and in proposing the toast he
would couple with it the names of those gentlemen present who had a
material interest in the line and would hereafter have to direct its
management. Amongst those gentlemen he saw his worthy friend
Mr Sherriff (Cheers), upon whom a great deal of the responsibility
for meeting the wants of the district rested.

The toast, 'Success to the Severn Valley Railway', was then drunk,
and Mr Sherriff rose to reply.

He said that it was very unfortunate that Colonel Forester, or
some other member of the Severn Valley board, was not present to
perform the task of returning thanks for the cordial way in which
they had drunk success to their railway. With the early career of the
Severn Valley Railway he was probably more ignorant than most of
the gentlemen around him and certainly more so than their honour-
able chairman, who had all along taken so active a part in the battle.
He (Mr Sherriff) knew nothing about it until some years ago when
Sir Morton Peto had requested him to make a report on the traffic
prospects of the line, so as to justify him in going into it as a shareholder. He (Mr Sherriff) made so good a report after an inspection of
the route proposed as justified Sir Morton, and later Mr Brassey, in
determining to take hold of the line. (Cheers) It was quite true that
Colonel Forester and other gentlemen had stood true to their colours,
through good report and through evil report, and he gave them due
honour for the course they had all taken. But the fact remained, he
considered, that but for Mr Brassey, who had invested nearly a

46

Opening

quarter of a million pounds in the railway, the district would have
been much longer without one. But now that the railway was an
accomplished thing, he trusted that they would wait patiently until
they obtained all the accommodation that was intended to be given
them. What was once a line on paper had become a line on terra
firma and he hoped that it would meet the wishes and expectations
of all who had taken it up.

It was a great satisfaction to the directors of the Severn Valley
Railway to see the manner in which the railway had been taken up by
the inhabitants of Bewdley and the district. (Cheers) He looked upon
it as a most favourable indication for the future. As they at Bewdley
had taken up the matter so well he trusted they would show their
continued interest in the working of the line, as, if the various
districts through which the railway passed would but look to it as
their own concern, and have a careful eye upon it, and, when they
saw any neglect, take care and report it to headquarters, he was sure
there would be less grumbling than on many other railways.
(Applause) He was sure the directors of the West Midland Railway
would always be delighted to hear any reasonable complaints and,
they might depend on their being remedied as far as possible. The
inhabitants must not regard the time-tables as issued for the first
month of operations as a settled arrangement with regard to the
trains to be run on the Severn Valley Railway. They must be aware
that they were compelled to run some trains or other but alterations
would, of course, be made and the operations of the line would, he
hoped, eventually be satisfactory to all concerned.

Mr W. C. Hemmings, in giving the toast, 'The health of Sir
Thomas Winnington, the Chairman', said that now that they had got
the facilities of railway accommodation he trusted that efforts would
be made by those to whom the arrangements had been deputed to
secure the comfort and convenience of those who might wish to travel.
As Mr Sherriff had kindly promised, they had only to complain
and should have everything they wanted ('No, no' and laughter).
He hoped that before next month, the trains would be made to run
with a little more facility and that instead of it taking one hour and
ten minutes to go from Bewdley to Worcester, they would be able to
go in half an hour, as they could from Kidderminster at the present
time. He did not make any complaint of this matter because he
knew that there was considerable difficulty experienced at the first
opening of a line and that it was a matter of trial and error.

Hemmings was confident that Bewdley would become more

47

prosperous on account of the railway. The town was delightfully situated, its poor rates were not high, and there was sufficient inducement within it for parties to become residents, and to open up a trade with the district. He thought that many would agree that it was a misfortune that no canal had been built near the town in the previous generation but this would be more than compensated by the arrival of the railway. The value of property would be enhanced, fresh faces would be continually seen among them, businesses would be opened and altogether the good old town would present quite a different appearance.

Sir Thomas Winnington replied in terms which contrived to be as self-effacing as they were expansive and proceeded to propose the health of the engineers of the railway. Sir John (or Mr as he then was) Fowler was not present and thus it fell to his assistant throughout the work, Henry Orlando Bridgman, to reply, expressing his best wishes for the prosperity of Bewdley and his confidence that its citizens would have no cause to regret the coming of the railway.

Other toasts – to the contractors, the City of Worcester, the West Midland Railway and the town of Stourport – were proposed and replied to. 'The town and trade of Stourport' was responded to by William Baldwin, an uncle of Stanley, who remarked that as the owner of one of the largest businesses in the area, an ironworks at Stourport, he anticipated that he would be as great a customer of the new line as he was of the existing railway system to the south and east.

Thus the Severn Valley Railway was launched amid the pleasure of achievement and in the hope of profit. Yet the whole history of the building of the line had been one of declining expectations. It is ironic that this area, so close to the birthplace of the industrial revolution, should have been without a railway for so long. The truth is, of course, that by the middle of the nineteenth century, the centres of industry had moved from the comparatively small and ancient towns where the transition from cottage crafts to organized mass manufacture had occurred, to the new cities which within the short space of fifty years had been begotten, reared and sustained by uninhibited industrial expansion. Even today, the appearance of towns such as Bewdley and Bridgnorth, shows that the height of their prosperity was reached long before the railway age.

Hemmings was perfectly right, from a commercial point of view, when he spoke of the 'misfortune that no canal had been built near the town' of Bewdley. The Staffordshire and Worcestershire canal, built seventy-five years before and partly with the intention of working in association with the River Severn, in effect drained the upper Severn valley of its old prosperity and Stourport alone burgeoned under its influence. It was Stourport, too, which had the benefit of the near-by stations at Hartlebury and Kidderminster – as was pointed out to the select committee on the 1853 Bill – before the Severn Valley line was built.

The pace of commercial life in the area was set by men like Pearce Baldwin and his family, ironfounders of Stourport and Wolverhampton, who had been one of the leading advocates of improved communications with the central Midlands and the north of England but, in this respect, the opening of the Kidderminster loop eighteen years later was a more significant event.

6
Operations

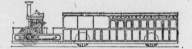

'The trains', Forester told his shareholders soon after the line was opened, 'of the West Midland Company have been run with great regularity.' In the earliest days the service on the Severn Valley line consisted of three trains between Shrewsbury and Hartlebury in each direction every day. There was no Sunday service during February 1862, the month after the opening, but thereafter there was one train in each direction. On weekdays there was also a morning train from Shrewsbury to Bridgnorth and back. All trains stopped at all stations, except for one train a day in each direction which did not stop at Linley. The journey time varied from 2 hours and 3 minutes to $2\frac{1}{4}$ hours. Connecting services at Hartlebury and Shrewsbury made Holyhead, Liverpool, Manchester, Birmingham and Bristol remarkably easy to reach and the 150 miles from Bridgnorth to London (Paddington) could be covered in 5 hours and 45 minutes; by the turn of the century this had improved to $4\frac{1}{2}$ hours, and the local service to five trains a day and two on Sundays.

The OW&W had become the constituent company of the West Midland Railway before the line was built. On 1 August 1863 the West Midland itself was dissolved and its obligations and powers vested in the GWR. For another seven years the West Midland shareholders retained vestiges of a separate identity until complete amalgamation was achieved in the Great Western Railway Act of 1872. Several directors of the West Midland joined the Great Western board: Edward Watkin, who had succeeded Sherriff as general manager of the WMR, William Fenton, the chairman, and John Parson among them, though Parson withered in the more sedate atmosphere of the Great Western boardroom and ended his career in disrepute.

The Severn Valley's absorption into the greatest railway company in the country expedited two plans which had been under discussion for some years: the Tenbury & Bewdley line, and the Kidderminster loop.

The Tenbury & Bewdley line, running from Bewdley, over the Severn by Dowles bridge, through the Wyre Forest to Neen Sollars, and thence along the valley of the River Teme and its tributary the Rea, to Tenbury Wells and linked to a junction with the Shrewsbury & Hereford main line at Wooferton, had a comparatively smooth history. The Severn Valley directors noted in February 1860 that the project had been well subscribed, mainly by residents along the proposed route. The enabling Act was passed in July that year, and the works completed quickly and peacefully by Brassey and Field, ready for opening on 13 August 1864.

The Kidderminster loop had a longer and less equable history. From the very earliest years of the Severn Valley Co., the proposal for an additional link between Bewdley and Kidderminster, a distance of only 3 miles, had been much canvassed. Next to the main line to London, via Worcester, the most alluring aspect of having a railway at all, as far as the commercial community was concerned, was direct access to Wolverhampton and Birmingham. The question had been raised before the committee on the 1853 Bill and was constantly discussed by the board. An initiative came from the West Midland Co. in February 1861 and on 26 June a special general meeting was held to approve the application for a Bill to construct the loop. Though this stretch of line as eventually built was only 3 miles and $31\frac{1}{2}$ chains in length, it was quite a difficult job, involving a large cutting and tunnel west of Foley Park. It was not until the GWR took over that the plan came to anything and even then it was six years in the building. During construction, by Messrs Crockett and Dickenson, there were a number of serious accidents, two of them fatal. In March 1876 two navvies – Matthew Jones and Henry Philips – were killed by a fall of earth while working in the Bewdley tunnel, and a third – John Pritchard – was buried by an earth slip in the cutting at the western approach to the tunnel the following autumn. The loop was opened on 1 June 1878. 'There will be no demonstration', observed the *Kidderminster Shuttle*, 'so far as the Railway Company are concerned, and the line has been so long in construction that the residents have lost the little enthusiasm they manifested when the work was commenced.'

The Kidderminster–Bewdley–Hartlebury triangle developed quite a reputation for the disastrous and gruesome during the 1890s: a Miss Jones was murdered by her lover during the journey from Hartlebury to Kidderminster, a deranged guard named Jenkins attempted to wreck a train while it was standing in Stourport station, and a little further up the line a woman threw herself in front of an advancing train but was rescued at grave personal risk by P.C. W. Hardwicke, who received a medal and an illuminated address from the Royal Humane Society.

In its early years under the GWR the line prospered. Though passenger traffic was never heavy, the many estates and large houses along the banks of the river ensured that services and facilities, such as the provision of equipment for unloading horses and carriages at several of the stations, were maintained at a high standard, though there was a gradual decline from the 1880s onwards. The hopes of the builders and engineers that they would make a substantial and enduring line were largely fulfilled and no large scale maintenance work was necessary until just before World War I.

After 1918, in a social climate totally remote from that in which the line was conceived and built, the GWR made considerable efforts to exploit the recreational aspects of the area. The 'Handy Aids' series of guide books included one on the Severn Valley under the sub-title 'Through the Land of the Lords Marchers from Shrewsbury to Worcester', which ran to five editions during the 1920s. Certainly, with the ever-growing industrial Midlands within easy reach by rail through the creeping suburbs of Birmingham, absorbing the old towns and dwindling countryside of south Staffordshire and north-east Worcestershire, the GWR had discovered an admirable and useful way of supplementing the returns on passenger traffic on the line. Excursion trains, mainly at weekends and on public holidays, grew in number and continued with great success right up to the closure of the line, as, indeed, they could again. The unmanned halts opened on the southern half of the line mainly to serve fishermen and ramblers were also quite successful.

But the surest and most profitable traffic on the line from its opening to the closure was coal, and the supply of the power stations at Buildwas and Stourport-on-Severn, built between the wars. At Stourport it was intended that it should be partly supplied by the Staffordshire and Worcestershire Canal, but deliveries of coal by this means dwindled and stopped altogether in 1945, so that the extensive sidings provided there have been used to the full ever since, holding their own against the challenge of road transport.

On 13 January 1928 the line's most spectacular derailment occurred, though fortunately without causing any serious injury to the four passengers in the train concerned. The 7.45 p.m. train from Shrewsbury was approaching Bridgnorth shortly after half past eight when it left the tracks. Two hundred and fifty yards or so of line was wrecked and the train finally stopped not far short of the northern entrance to High Town tunnel. The engine, a 2-6-2 Prairie tank, no. 5508, which was only about a year old, was examined by the Great Western's chief mechanical engineer, Mr C. B. Collett, who, the *Bridgnorth Journal* observed on the occasion of his visit, was 'the main figure in the evolution of the famous steam engine "King George V", now on exhibition at Baltimore, Ohio'. The report of the enquiry into the accident referred to the speed of the train as a possible factor but found that the principal cause was the decayed state of some of the sleepers on that section of the track, and made recommendations as to future inspection and maintenance.

During World War II, with maximum utilization of the entire railway system, the status and importance of the Severn Valley line as a through route went up. Formerly classed as a 'light' route, it was raised to a 'blue', that is, a line permitted to carry engines with an axle loading of up to $17\frac{1}{2}$ tons, though some heavier engines were seen on troop trains from time to time. The line also served two important RAF installations at Bridgnorth and Hartlebury and, by way of the Wyre Forest branch, the Admiralty installations at Ditton Priors, up towards Ludlow.

The operational history of the line has been marred by two fatal accidents, involving the deaths of four people. It is ironical, in view of the special care taken by the Board of Trade inspectors during planning and building, over the location of level crossings, that the two accidents should have occurred on the same crossing, and all the more unfortunate in so far as both road and rail traffic over it were exceedingly light. The crossing, near Northwood Halt on the east bank of the river between Bewdley and Arley, was marked by the usual warning signs, 'STOP LOOK LISTEN', and engines signified their approach round the bend from the direction of Bewdley by blasts on the whistle. In the first accident, in August 1947, a woman and her small daughter were passengers in a car hit by a goods train and killed; in the second, in August 1964, an empty coal train returning to Alveley carried a car 300 yards along the track, killing two of the four passengers in it.

Table II. Traffic Statistics of the Severn Valley Railway, 1903–1938

Station*	Year	Passenger train traffic			Freight train traffic		Total revenue £
		Tickets issued	Parcels & milk desp.	Revenue £	Rec'd & desp. tons	Revenue £	
Stourport-on-Severn	1903	29,300	21,338	3,155	76,174	24,437	27,592
	1913	36,902	32,380	4,300	88,667	31,006	35,306
	1923	37,736	22,474	6,286	96,711	49,168	55,454
	1929	21,846	25,260	4,733	134,403	62,859	67,592
	1930	18,510	24,515	4,142	124,495	54,484	58,626
	1931	19,235	26,124	4,202	123,042	59,075	63,277
	1932	16,836	25,153	3,946	111,488	51,116	55,062
	1933	17,137	28,787	4,176	133,929	61,403	65,579
	1934	17,112	31,063	4,079	153,258	72,346	76,425
	1935	17,690	32,072	3,982	158,949	77,922	81,904
	1936	16,746	36,160	4,156	152,276	71,715	75,871
	1937	15,749	35,494	3,490	153,781	77,105	80,595
	1938	16,269	36,566	4,078	130,922	61,178	65,256
Bewdley	1903	63,131	15,577	4,296	16,588	5,076	9,372
	1913	82,475	19,845	4,702	17,020	4,074	8,776
	1923	92,463	16,783	7,584	20,171	7,553	15,137
	1929	92,479	17,812	6,202	20,201	8,875	15,077
	1930	88,763	14,840	5,251	19,323	7,812	13,063
	1931	69,627	14,706	4,922	20,599	9,227	14,149
	1932	56,206	13,689	4,042	16,907	7,180	11,222
	1933	56,012	15,578	4,007	15,158	6,802	10,809
	1934	55,051	15,834	4,061	14,797	6,679	10,740
	1935	61,135	16,093	3,988	13,668	5,920	9,908
	1936	63,262	16,300	3,896	14,457	6,931	10,827
	1937	66,925	16,001	4,164	13,357	5,627	9,701
	1938	60,251	14,120	3,748	10,874	3,833	7,581
Arley	1903	17,295	2,453	914	881	178	1,092
	1913	15,796	3,219	761	1,399	301	1,062
	1923	12,898	1,341	862	1,828	996	1,858
	1929	11,200	1,626	752	312	129	881
	1930	9,682	1,024	614	119	62	676
	1931	9,330	996	522	113	64	586
	1932	8,370	815	456	3,347	525	981
	1933	8,663	997	477	54	47	524
	1934	8,920	1,037	504	149	96	600
	1935	9,864	977	495	71	54	549
	1936	10,231	1,228	518	109	78	596
	1937	10,759	1,255	549	46	21	570
	1938	11,623	926	526	44	24	550
Highley	1903	17,559	3,247	1,185	140,939	24,372	25,557
	1913	29,030	7,308	2,515	219,271	32,774	35,289
	1923	22,234	4,873	2,838	175,115	41,695	44,533
	1929	37,655	6,015	2,853	179,452	29,060	31,913
	1930	32,289	5,787	2,483	185,993	29,745	32,228
	1931	24,203	6,268	2,008	166,634	26,019	28,027
	1932	22,238	6,137	1,937	177,249	26,146	28,083
	1933	21,548	6,237	1,877	177,543	24,932	26,809
	1934	20,301	6,140	1,982	188,262	26,394	28,376
	1935	23,925	6,051	1,794	182,971	25,245	27,039
	1936	25,108	6,232	1,870	193,693	27,829	29,699
	1937	23,400	6,457	1,822	166,607	24,123	25,945
	1938	21,335	6,584	1,606	154,202	23,128	24,734
Hampton Loade	1903	9,967	2,691	760	1,488	631	1,391
	1913	10,350	3,076	579	4,632	1,270	1,849
	1923	9,077	3,117	778	900	599	1,377
	1929	5,966	5,085	734	936	401	1,135
	1930	5,619	6,663	849	671	211	1,060
	1931	5,410	6,417	760	252	130	890
	1932	5,011	5,187	620	85	56	676
	1933	4,704	1,183	350	335	147	497
	1934	4,781	857	323	491	149	472
	1935	3,110	848	293	801	181	474
	1936	4,919	827	279	360	148	427
	1937	5,584	733	305	245	82	387
	1938	5,116	659	304	555	201	505

Operations

Station*	Year	Passenger train traffic			Freight train traffic		Total revenue £
		Tickets issued	Parcels & milk desp.	Revenue £	Rec'd & desp. tons	Revenue £	
Eardington	1903	5,944	778	290	1,493	609	899
	1913	6,690	961	311	1,704	464	775
	1923	5,267	2,259	389	2,355	1,275	1,664
	1929	3,926	542	172	1,361	550	722
	1930	4,113	506	156	1,418	384	540
	1931	4,240	435	167	694	216	383
	1932	3,902	484	177	854	251	428
	1933	3,361	438	150	604	217	367
	1934	2,490	530	138	802	265	403
	1935	2,496	549	168	1,069	279	447
	1936	2,159	519	153	1,126	348	501
	1937	2,316	447	143	951	261	404
	1938	2,075	277	90	1,434	273	303
Bridgnorth	1903	52,796	40,029	9,318	46,455	15,536	24,854
	1913	69,062	48,730	9,802	50,213	16,470	26,272
	1923	40,127	44,603	10,231	49,210	28,320	38,551
	1929	25,355	38,512	6,953	49,025	25,114	32,067
	1930	29,298	37,177	6,244	54,803	23,328	29,572
	1931	20,151	35,819	5,437	45,132	19,259	24,696
	1932	18,285	35,088	4,873	32,949	15,883	20,756
	1933	17,232	38,478	4,755	31,651	15,708	20,463
	1934	16,746	40,345	4,856	31,380	16,378	21,234
	1935	15,960	41,083	3,488	32,637	16,370	19,858
	1936	16,074	40,695	3,598	32,969	16,968	20,566
	1937	14,766	38,353	3,373	31,356	16,213	19,586
	1938	13,500	37,800	3,190	29,141	15,367	18,557
Linley	1903	5,280	1,506	403	159	71	474
	1913	4,780	1,537	433	772	149	612
	1923	4,569	836	462	212	51	513
	1929	3,805	946	313	345	124	437
	1930	3,542	763	279	460	145	424
	1931	3,591	743	266	328	85	351
	1932	3,843	822	300	287	63	363
	1933	3,482	931	303	253	90	393
	1934	4,441	1,092	347	421	208	555
	1935	4,037	874	304	405	219	523
	1936	4,285	790	338	102	93	431
	1937	3,735	681	247	42	79	326
	1938	3,750	722	263	454	201	464
Coalport	1903	7,906	1,325	493	11,021	3,820	4,313
	1913	6,622	1,257	490	6,823	1,850	2,340
	1923	8,984	1,885	754	9,253	3,857	4,611
	1929	6,721	2,160	553	8,060	2,961	3,514
	1930	7,012	2,485	572	7,681	2,854	3,426
	1931	5,810	1,959	506	5,880	2,391	2,897
	1932	5,096	1,401	433	4,529	1,857	2,290
	1933	5,771	690	412	5,950	2,750	3,162
	1934	6,787	909	513	3,971	1,330	1,843
	1935	7,373	545	415	3,404	1,239	1,654
	1936	6,398	1,232	439	4,913	1,832	2,261
	1937	6,301	1,198	417	5,513	1,657	2,074
	1938	5,741	1,257	366	4,937	1,771	2,137
Ironbridge & Broseley	1903	29,845	19,240	3,314	75,457	24,895	28,209
	1913	24,247	19,681	2,719	65,253	18,948	21,667
	1923	32,384	17,827	4,742	62,216	29,153	33,895
	1929	24,912	17,603	4,020	59,847	27,192	31,212
	1930	25,574	17,544	3,726	53,593	23,216	26,942
	1931	25,684	17,755	3,695	51,771	21,923	25,618
	1932	21,607	19,472	3,582	45,503	19,239	22,821
	1933	19,195	21,354	3,276	40,780	18,322	21,596
	1934	22,230	22,647	3,493	38,006	17,643	21,136
	1935	27,874	22,295	3,234	30,452	15,407	18,646
	1936	28,648	23,483	3,317	30,192	15,793	19,110
	1937	26,702	24,262	3,052	31,812	15,375	18,427
	1938	23,637	23,712	3,151	27,170	11,969	15,120

Operations

Station*	Year	Passenger train traffic Tickets issued	Parcels & milk desp.	Revenue £	Freight train traffic Rec'd & desp. tons	Revenue £	Total revenue £
Buildwas	1903	9,693	1,258	598	3,831	700	1,298
	1913	9,601	2,445	582	3,980	600	1,182
	1923	7,098	1,023	432	3,838	755	1,187
	1929	7,151	1,681	546	41,085	3,837	4,383
	1930	8,529	2,016	655	43,731	12,415	13,070
	1931	10,710	1,178	715	43,062	15,802	16,517
	1932	8,923	1,618	850	31,317	6,048	6,898
	1933	5,983	1,029	489	49,?9	4,105	4,594
	1934	5,966	964	473	149,780	7,828	8,301
	1935	6,483	991	450	198,216	18,690	19,140
	1936	7,102	1,195	492	285,032	21,569	22,061
	1937	6,799	966	408	335,241	17,124	17,532
	1938	7,720	1,465	561	324,330	23,092	24,555
Cressage	1903	13,514	2,692	979	5,768	1,329	2,308
	1913	14,353	4,109	1,064	5,305	1,449	2,513
	1923	12,558	11,119	1,871	4,020	1,852	3,723
	1929	8,457	3,849	1,040	4,636	1,946	2,986
	1930	7,902	4,451	1,017	4,291	1,770	2,787
	1931	7,104	4,270	667	2,532	1,197	2,064
	1932	6,371	3,631	760	2,669	1,011	1,771
	1933	5,852	3,985	736	3,225	1,081	1,817
	1934	6,137	2,519	665	4,366	1,660	2,325
	1935	6,339	2,288	601	5,761	1,936	2,537
	1936	6,197	2,230	555	4,960	1,818	2,273
	1937	5,535	2,114	523	4,519	1,643	2,166
	1938	5,161	2,024	447	2,399	1,023	1,470
Berrington	1903	16,855	4,695	881	8,275	1,951	2,832
	1913	14,073	6,989	989	7,992	2,053	3,042
	1923	9,014	5,380	973	5,042	2,379	3,352
	1929	7,266	4,599	708	7,480	2,098	2,806
	1930	6,091	3,472	635	6,977	2,187	2,822
	1931	5,600	2,533	477	6,904	1,847	2,324
	1932	4,824	2,696	507	6,300	1,591	2,098
	1933	4,811	2,807	456	6,085	1,362	1,818
	1934	4,865	3,181	476	6,686	1,719	2,195
	1935	5,506	3,359	435	8,120	2,287	2,722
	1936	4,953	3,849	351	7,953	2,087	2,438
	1937	4,100	2,602	331	7,006	2,003	2,334
	1938	3,348	2,967	303	6,086	1,774	2,077

* Burlish Halt included with Stourport-on-Severn; Northwood Halt with Bewdley; Jackfield Halt with Ironbridge & Broseley; Cound Halt with Cressage and Berrington.

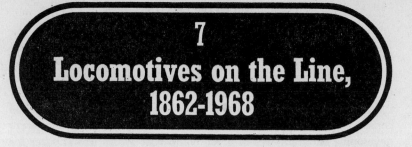

7
Locomotives on the Line, 1862-1968

A fascinating parade of steam locomotives ran up and down the Severn Valley line in the years between 1862 and 1969, when the last British Railways colliery train worked from the Highley mine of the National Coal Board to the main line of the Western Region at Kidderminster. To be absolutely precise and satisfy the pedants, the short stretch of line from Hartlebury to the sidings of the great 'A' and 'B' electric power stations of the nationalized authority at Stourport-on-Severn (the proposal for a third, 'C' Station, an inland nuclear station, was mercifully defeated on planning grounds in 1970) is sensibly kept open and dieselized traction hauls the coal trains to the entrance to the power station sidings, where several steam locomotives, saddle tanks of the electricity authority, ply on shunting duties. Otherwise, Severn Valley steam traction is confined to the growing stock of locomotives operated by the Severn Valley Railway Co. on scheduled passenger and ancillary services between Bridgnorth and Hampton Loade.

When the railway was first opened in 1862 it linked two major railway centres, Shrewsbury in the north and Worcester in the south, the latter by way of the Hartlebury junction of the OW&W main line, and at Worcester itself by way of the Worcester & Hereford Railway and the Birmingham & Gloucester Railway via the Lickey incline near Bromsgrove. At Shrewsbury four major routes met, each operated by a different company: the Shrewsbury & Birmingham line to the south-east, the Shrewsbury & Hereford line to the south-west, the Shrewsbury & Chester line to the north, and the Stafford

Union Railway to the east. Into this maelstrom obtruded the Severn Valley line in 1862, with an attractive and promising traffic potential.

The decade during which the Severn Valley line operated prior to its absorption into the Great Western system was important for large-scale amalgamations and takeovers which were the logical consequence of the mania of the 1840s. The great companies were developing their empires in fierce competition with one another for routes and traffic. The growth of the GWR from the Midlands was particularly remarkable in the 1860s, taking over the Birkenhead Railway jointly with the LNWR and operated by the two companies until 1923, and then by the GWR and LMSR until nationalization. Other GWR acquisitions were the constituent companies of the West Midland Railway formed in 1860. Thus, by the late 1860s, the Great Western reached the Mersey by way of Paddington, Didcot, Oxford, Banbury, Birmingham, Wolverhampton, Shrewsbury and Chester to Birkenhead, a distance of about 230 miles. Of course, the LNWR had the shorter route to Liverpool, via Crewe. Because of these mergers, the inventory of locomotives taken over by the GWR was greatly diversified, and was further complicated by dual-gauging. Brunel's Great Western main line from London to Bristol, with many associated branches, having been built on the broad gauge and most of the other railways in Britain on the narrow and now standard 4 feet 8½ inch gauge. Over increasing lengths of line between 1840 and the final extinction of the broad gauge in 1892 there were three rails, or dual-gauging, with all the attendant and formidable and costly 'conversion' requirements for locomotives and rolling stock, the transhipment of passengers and freight, wherever and whenever the broad gauge met the narrow. But in 1862, the year of the opening of the Severn Valley line, the Great Western was on the brink of an extraordinary split over its own gauge. Having won the battle to take over the Shrewsbury & Birmingham line against the LNWR, it was required by the enabling Act that the line north of Wolverhampton should remain narrow gauge.

This situation influenced locomotive construction, and in 1864, when Joseph Armstrong took over from Sir Daniel Gooch as first locomotive, carriage and wagon superintendent of the GWR, he established his headquarters at Swindon, where the new works was to be built following the defeat of plans to build it at Oxford, where the university authorities declaimed against industrialization of their academic lives. His brother George was left to run the other great works centre at Stafford Road, Wolverhampton. Thus, in essence, Swindon and Wolverhampton became respectively the centres of broad and narrow gauge locomotive design and construction. Though the last new broad gauge engines were built at Swindon in 1866, apart from the rebuilding and restoration of existing Gooch locomotives of the earlier Great Western period between 1840 and 1865, right down to the conversion of the gauges in 1892, the famous Gooch 8 foot singles kept in the forefront of fast passenger locomotion, a class which justly earned the name 'aristocrats of the line', comparable in quality, dignity and efficiency to the Patrick Stirling 8 foot singles, to be described later.

A miscellany of Wolverhampton types ran on the Severn Valley line in its first thirty or forty years. There were the engines with 2-2-2 wheel arrangement like no. 110 which emerged from Wolverhampton in 1862, the 2-4-0 tender locomotives, which first came out in 1863, the 0-6-0 goods engines in the late sixties and, of course, the little tank engines later to develop by logical and evolutionary processes into the numerous GWR tank engine types so well known all over the system in the following hundred years. They originated in the Armstrong saddle tank (0-6-0ST), of the 302 class which emerged from the Wolverhampton works a couple of years after the Severn Valley line's opening and, in all the years to closure in 1962, these tank engines, the 0-6-0ST and the famous GWR pannier tanks in their manifold varieties, the Prairies, little and big, with their many modifications, the four-coupled, 'in-front' passenger tank engines of the 0-4-2T wheel formation which were still being built as late as the 1930s, and several of which are operating today on the Dart Valley line in Devonshire. And the 2-4-0T wheel formation, and the Barnums, 2-4-0 tender locomotives, were employed on nearly every railway in Britain for main-line passenger work, as in the case of the famous Jumbo type 2-4-0 of the LNWR. The GWR, in broad and narrow gauges, produced substantial numbers of these Barnums at Swindon and Wolverhampton, including the 717 class single framed, the 439 class, also single framed, the 149 class double framed, and the 3501 class originally built for Severn tunnel working. There were also the true Barnums, the 3206 class and, originating in Armstrong's 439 class, the 3232 class of which William Dean built forty at Swindon, with bigger boilers than had been fitted previously, 6 foot 8½ inch driving wheels, and 17½ inch inside cylinders. A fine photograph of no. 3244 of this 3232 class departing from Bewdley station on the Severn Valley line at the turn of the century, is reproduced in this book.

Of course in the early years there were numerous antiquated locomotives built by Fairbairn, by Kitson, by Hawthorn, or by Beyer Peacock, taken over by the West Midland Railway, rebuilt at Wolverhampton and used on the Severn Valley line. Two venerable 2-4-0s, nos 106 and 107, originally built by Fairbairn in 1845 for the Birkenhead Railway and rebuilt and renumbered at Wolverhampton in the 1870s, ended their working lives on the line in 1900 and 1902 respectively.

The 0-6-0 Dean goods worked on the line with its predecessor, the 0-6-0 Beyer tender engine. No. 338 of the Beyer 322 class is illustrated shunting at Bewdley in about 1925 when it was already half a century old. William Dean's 3201 class first appeared in 1883 and continued for fourteen years. Though usually single framed there were double-framed versions. The class evolved through the 2400 and 2500 series to Collett's 2251 class, which had a wider cab and improved protection for the crew against the elements, and culminated in Hawksworth's 3200 class, a splendid example of which, no. 3205, is running on Severn Valley metals today. Thus, this locomotive is a direct descendant of William Dean's renowned goods engine of 1883, affectionately known to steam locomotive men as the 'Dean goods'.

Great Western engines of the Victorian era included the famous 'Dukes', named after the first of the class, 'Duke of Cornwall', outside-framed 4-4-0s, progenitors of the 'Bulldogs', the 'Flowers' and the 'Cities'. All were four-coupled express locomotives, responsible for the crack Great Western expresses of their day, built before the great increase of passenger train weights in Edwardian days made necessary the succeeding generation of six-coupled, outside-cylinder Great Western express engines of the 'Saint', the 'Star', the 'Castle' and the 'King' classes, and the mixed traffic 'Halls', 'Manors' and 'Granges', so many of which have been preserved in all their former splendour and saved from breakers' yards. 'Dukes' were working on the Severn Valley line as late as World War II, notably no. 3254, 'Cornubia', which was shedded at Kidderminster, no. 3284, 'Isle of Jersey', shedded at Stourbridge, and the by then un-named no. 3276, originally called 'Dartmoor', shedded at Shrewsbury during the war. (No. 3254, originally no. 3255, built Swindon, July 1895, withdrawn, June 1950; no. 3284, built Swindon, April 1899, withdrawn, April 1951; no. 3276, built Swindon, March 1897, withdrawn, November 1949.)

The 'Dukes' were launched in 1893, the first ten of which were the following:

Locomotives on the Line, 1862–1968

3252 Duke of Cornwall	3257 Guinevere
3253 Pendennis Castle	3258 King Arthur
3254 Boscawen	3259 The Lizard
3255 Cornubia	3260 Merlin
3256 Excalibur	3261 Mount Edgcumbe

So successful were they that thirty more followed, all being in main line service by 1899:

3262 Powderham	3277 Earl of Devon
3263 Sir Lancelot	3278 Eddystone
3264 St Anthony	3279 Exmoor
3265 St Germans	3280 Falmouth
3266 St Ives	3281 Fowey
3267 St Michael	3282 Marlstone
3268 Tamar	3283 Mounts Bay
3269 Tintagel	3284 Isle of Jersey
3270 Trevethick	3285 St Erth
3271 Tre Pol and Pen	3286 St Just
3272 Amyas	3287 St Agnes
3273 Armorel	3288 Tresco
3274 Cornishman	3289 Trefusis
3275 Chough	3290 Torbay
3276 Dartmoor	3291 Tregenna

All forty names were chosen to enhance the romanticism of the West Country and the lore of the Duchy of Cornwall, the 'Cornish Riviera' and 'Glorious Devon', which the GWR so largely succeeded throughout all their advertising and publicity in turning to such excellent commercial advantage.

Descendants of the 'Dukes' were the sturdy, resilient 'Bulldog' class, named throughout and including among their considerable number the names of two members of the Baldwin family: 3363 'Alfred Baldwin', built January 1903, withdrawn October 1949 and 3701 (renumbered 3411 in 1912) 'Stanley Baldwin', built April 1906 and withdrawn October 1938. Later there was the 'Castle' class engine no. 5063, 'Earl Baldwin', built in June 1937 and withdrawn in February 1965, thus commemorating two generations of this great Worcestershire family who served as directors of the GWR.

All the romantic names first given to the 'Dukes' in the nineties were changed around in later years. 'Pendennis Castle', for example, originally 'Duke' no. 3253, one of the 'Western hill climbers' built for

Rattery, Dainton and Wellington Banks and the like on the main line, had its name attached to the even more famous 'Castle' class engine in 1923. The 'Dukedogs', also known on the Severn Valley line in the forties and fifties were derived from the original 'Dukes'. Called 'Dukedogs' because they were an amalgam of 'Dukes' and 'Bulldogs', these engines were really built for the Cambrian section of the GWR, from Whitchurch and Oswestry to Welshpool and on to the Cambrian coast at Aberystwyth, often hauling the express of that name on the last, hilly stages of its journey from Paddington. Twenty-nine 'Dukedogs' were built at Swindon between 1933 and 1939, and an earlier prototype locomotive was added; many of these thirty surviving until the end of steam on British Railways. One 'Dukedog', a fine and glamorous reminder of the Western years of 'Dukes' and 'Bulldogs', is preserved on the Bluebell line, no. 3217, 'Earl of Berkeley', and is pictured in this book. The engine was built at Swindon in March 1938, with the frames of no. 3425 (a 1906 'Bulldog') and fittings from no. 3258, 'The Lizard' (an 1895 'Duke'). No. 3217 officially replaced no. 3258 but its 'Duke'-type boiler was not in fact from that engine. No. 3217 was allocated the name 'Earl of Berkeley' but due to a change of policy never carried it. After its preservation, it was decided to put the original intention into practice and the appropriate nameplates were obtained from the GWR 'Castle' class locomotive which carried them.

Occasionally a 'Manor' class light 4-6-0 appeared on the Severn Valley line and very suitable they were for mixed freight working. Numbered from 7800 as GWR engines by C. B. Collett, they weighed 68 tons 18 cwt in working order and could generally operate in areas forbidden to 'Granges' and 'Halls'. Otherwise, in the last thirty years of Great Western working, the Severn Valley line saw few tender engines other than the 'Moguls' of the 4300 series, and variations in the 5300, 6300, 7300, 8300 and 9300 series, and an occasional 2-8-0 working the heavy colliery trains from Highley to the coal-burning power stations at Buildwas and Stourport.

From 1870 until the end of steam, the GWR favoured the 0-6-0T wheel arrangement for hundreds of her tank engines, earlier the saddles (S.T.) and latterly the panniers. It was the panniers that epitomized Great Western individuality. Certainly the GWR was the most extensive user of this wheel arrangement and in its last days, they were running all over the system in the 5700 class with associates from the earlier 2700, 3600, 4600 and 9600 classes and eventually with the superb panniers of the 9400 and 1500 classes. The 1600 class of pannier tank, with 4 foot 1½ inch wheels, was said to be a throw-back to the 2021 class of saddle tank built at Wolverhampton in the 1870s. But it was the very powerful 'super-panniers' of the Hawks-worth 1500 class, the last pure GWR design to emerge from Swindon before nationalization, which steal the limelight. Weighing 58 tons in working order, the second of her class, no. 1501, is preserved on the Severn Valley line today. She is owned by the Warwickshire Industrial Preservation Group and was rescued in 1969 from becom-ing derelict at the Keresley colliery of the National Coal Board. The finest example of a pannier tank – ex-GWR no. 5786 – is owned by the Worcester Locomotive Society and is now kept at Hereford alongside 'King George V', formerly GWR no. 6000. Nos 1501 and 5786 are illustrated in this book as preserved locomotives, and both have worked latterly on the Severn Valley line.

The GWR 'beasts of burden' were, by common consent, the Prairie tanks in the 3100 series and, with variations, the 4100, 5100, 6100 and 8100 series. The GWR had a great love for them for general utility and branch-line working. Two splendid examples of the small Prairie are no. 4555 and no. 4566, operating vivaciously on the Dart Valley and Severn Valley lines respectively. Both were built at Swindon in 1924 and are now fully restored.

Between the wars a high percentage of all GWR engines were 0-6-0T panniers and 2-6-2T Prairies, large and small, and 'heavies', such as the 2-8-0T and by adaptation the 2-8-2T, for coal and other mineral traffic, particularly in South Wales. In the years after the war until closure, most of the work on the Severn Valley line was done by former GWR pannier and Prairie tanks, aided occasionally by BR standard 2-6-2T class 3MT 82XXX engines and later by 2-6-2Ts of the Ivatt class 2MT, series 41XXX. Very occasionally, on a heavy mineral train, a BR 2-10-0 class 9F, identical to no. 92220 'Evening Star' – the last BR steam engine to be built at Swindon in 1960 – and a former LMS 2-8-0 class 8F, identical to no. 8233 working on the railway today, were observed on the line working to and from the power stations at Buildwas and Stourport.

8
Closure and Revival

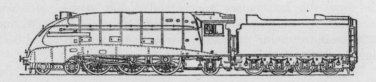

After nationalization, the Severn Valley line, along with most of the Great Western, passed to the Western Region of British Railways. There was no immediate effect on operations. The long-term prospects of the railway were affected more by general economic conditions than by the change in management and ownership. In relation to the volume of traffic, in particular passenger traffic, it was an exorbitantly expensive line to maintain, particularly on account of several serious landslips during the first few years after nationalization. One of them, at Jackfield in 1954, moved the line downwards and sideways over a distance of 400 yards, necessitating large-scale repairs and a speed limit of 5 m.p.h. Otherwise, little general maintenance and restoration was carried out, although the track over the Victoria bridge was relaid, complete with new sleepers and fresh ballast, in 1954.

Apart from these events, the fifteen years between nationalization and the transfer of the line to the London Midland Region for a few months before the beginning of closure in 1963, were very quiet. British Railways pursued much the same policy as the GWR had done for years in using the line as a repository for the remnants of dwindling classes of engine and older carriage stock. Diesel multiple units began to appear on the line after 1956, in addition to the railcars which had been in use since the 1940s. The volume of passenger traffic remained comparatively as good as it had ever been, bearing in mind that the population of the area was fairly static, and in spite of the challenge of private cars and the more frequent and versatile bus services. But there was nothing special to save the line from the Transport Act 1962 or prevent its closure.

The last scheduled passenger trains between Bewdley and Sutton Bridge ran on 7 September 1963, followed by the end of through freight services on 30 November. South of Alveley, the line remained open for coal traffic from the colliery, but north of Buildwas the track was lifted in 1965, and later south as far as Bridgnorth. The Hartlebury–Bewdley section, and the Kidderminster loop, originally scheduled for closure in April 1969, remained in operation until January 1970, following action by the Transport Users Consultative Committee. All services on the Tenbury branch ended in 1964. The line was raised and severed from the east bank of the river by the dismantling of the Dowles bridge, which had stood for exactly one hundred years. Fortunately, the activities of the preservationists have prevented any such drastic action over the Victoria bridge during the two years that it has been unused.

It is unlikely that the Severn Valley line could have been kept open under any reasonable terms. Even today, the area is not densely populated and by most standards other means of public transport are good. But with certain economies – the earlier introduction of railcars, the conversion of some stations to unmanned halts and more imaginative promotion of the railway in connection with recreational pursuits – could have made it a less obvious candidate for closure.

The closure of branch lines and the destruction of works, together with the passing of steam, has given enormous impetus to existing preservation societies and has begotten more. Among these is the Severn Valley Railway Society, which occupied the line until 6 December 1969 when it merged with the Severn Valley Railway Co., and which originated in the mind of a Kidderminster maintenance fitter, Mr Keith Beddoes. On his initiative, a meeting of about fifty people at the Cooper's Arms in Kidderminster on 6 July 1965 transformed the idea into more substantial form. An inspection of the line between Hampton Loade and Bridgnorth on Sunday 25 July revealed demolition work to be imminent there. Contact was made with British Railways immediately and work stopped within a matter of days. A further meeting of the society early in August resolved to try to lease the line between Bridgnorth and Hampton Loade and operate steam-hauled trains on it, partly for the benefit of members and enthusiasts, partly as a tourist attraction and possibly, in due course, as a contribution to local transport facilities. In the event, British Railways were unwilling to lease the line but were ready to consider an offer for outright purchase. The society accepted the challenge and after a survey and valuation of the line, a price of £25,000 was agreed in February 1966. Before the application for a

Severn Valley Railway Company Limited

Summer Timetable 1971

Saturdays		\multicolumn{9}{c}{10 April–30th October 1971}								
		D	D	A	D		B		B	C
Bridgnorth	dep.	09.00	11.00	12.00	13.00	14.00	15.00	16.00	17.00	18.00
Eardington	dep.	09.08	11.08	12.10	13.08	14.10	15.10	16.10	17.10	18.10
Hampton Loade	arr.	09.15	11.15	12.20	13.15	14.20	15.20	16.20	17.20	18.20
Hampton Loade	dep.	09.30	11.30	12.35	13.30	14.35	15.35	16.35	17.35	18.35
Eardington	dep.	09.38	11.38	12.45	13.38	14.45	15.45	16.45	17.45	18.45
Bridgnorth	arr.	09.45	11.45	12.55	13.45	14.55	15.55	16.55	17.55	18.55

Sundays & Bank Holidays		\multicolumn{8}{c}{11 April–31st October 1971}							
			A		B		B	C
Bridgnorth	dep.	12.00	13.00	14.00	15.00	16.00	17.00	18.00
Eardington	dep.	12.10	13.10	14.10	15.10	16.10	17.10	18.10
Hampton Loade	arr.	12.20	13.20	14.20	15.20	16.20	17.20	18.20
Hampton Loade	dep.	12.35	13.35	14.35	15.35	16.35	17.35	18.35
Eardington	dep.	12.45	13.45	14.45	15.45	16.45	17.45	18.45
Bridgnorth	arr.	12.55	13.55	14.55	15.55	16.55	17.55	18.55

Notes: A – only runs at Bank Holiday weekends, i.e. Easter, Spring and Summer.
B – will run during June, July and August and at Bank Holiday weekends, but at other periods only as required and may be a Diesel Railcar.
C – only runs during June, July and August and at Bank Holiday weekends.
D – Diesel Railcar shoppers' service.

Light Railway Order it was necessary to form a limited company and it was for this reason among others that the Severn Valley Railway Co. was formed and incorporated on 24 May 1967. In the meantime, the enterprise had attracted some formidable champions, including Mr Richard Dunn, who played a prominent part in the many battles which had to be fought before the grant of the second Light Railway Order in May 1970.

On 1 June 1967 contracts were exchanged on the sale of the stretch of line actually owned by the company (from Bridgnorth to Alveley, although it is only operated as far south as Hampton Loade at present) and the battle for the first Light Railway Order began in the face of determined opposition by the Shropshire County Council, initially the Chelmarsh Parish Council, and certain uninformed individuals. Repeated attempts to reach an agreement with the former were fruitless and it became obvious that a full-scale public enquiry was inevitable, if only because of the intransigence of some of the personalities .involved. Although an extraordinary meeting with the chairman and chief officers of the Council was held on 10 July 1968, this resulted in stalemate.

The public enquiry took place on 1 and 2 October 1968 in the no. 1 Assize Court at the Shirehall in Shrewsbury, before Mr T. H. Lewis, O.B.E. The company and the society were represented by Mr Richard Dunn. The second afternoon of the enquiry was devoted to a trip on the line from Bridgnorth to Bewdley, which, in perfect weather and conditions, clearly impressed the Ministry of Transport inspector. He reported accordingly, although the line was still not to open for another twenty months, when the third Minister of Transport to deal with the matter, the Rt Hon. Fred Mulley, M.P., finally gave his consent on 4 December 1969.

The procedure followed is elaborate. For a new line to be opened, it is necessary to obtain a private Act of parliament (e.g. Severn Valley Railway Acts of 1853, 1855 and 1856). To reopen an existing public railway to passenger traffic, two Light Railway Orders are required, the first on the application of British Rail to downgrade the line, the second to transfer all the rights and obligations of the line to the purchaser, under the provisions of the Light Railways Acts, 1896 and 1912 and the Railways Act 1921. Before this, however, the government requires surplus railway land to be offered to the local authority. Furthermore, the promoters of a private railway must answer a very detailed, technical questionnaire from Colonel J. R. H. Robertson, O.B.E., the Chief Inspecting Officer of Railways at the Ministry of Transport, as to the proposed mode of operation and maintenance of the line. The contract to purchase the line will be conditional upon the grant of the two Light Railway Orders, and will only (now) deal with the real property – the fixtures and fittings, trackwork and signalling equipment being sold separately. The grant of the second Light Railway Order is dependent upon a final inspection of the line and everything on it, and will regulate such matters as the speed of trains and axle loading, and the effective date of the latter is dependent upon the completion of the purchase of the line, that is to say, payment in full. Any serious objection to the first application will result in a public enquiry by the minister.

The hearing at Shrewsbury in October 1968 succeeded in bringing the suspicions of the Shropshire County Council to a head, although they are even now not resolved. Nevertheless, 6½ miles of line are in splendid working order and attracted tens of thousands of visitors during the summer of 1970.

For the future, the Severn Valley Railway Co. faces two great challenges: the proposed Bridgnorth by-pass, and the purchase and operation of the remainder of the line to the south as far as Foley Park halt, near Kidderminster. The by-pass, which is a highly controversial issue even among those who have no interest in the railway, threatens, as planned at present, to sever the line just south of Bridgnorth station unless the company can accommodate it with a bridge, which would involve a crippling financial burden. The purchase of the remainder of the line is an equally formidable problem. Though in first-class condition, it is approximately twice the length of the part at present in operation and will cost three times as much, but if a satisfactory purchase is concluded, the prospects of the line will be vastly enhanced and a rail link between Bridgnorth and Kidderminster re-established.

Thus in years to come, a new station may arise from the present British Railways one at Kidderminster, bearing the legend once displayed at Hartlebury:

CHANGE HERE FOR THE SEVERN VALLEY LINE

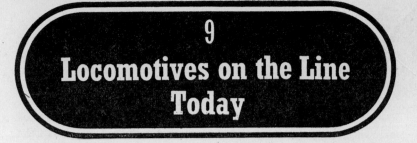

9
Locomotives on the Line Today

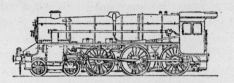

The preservation of steam locomotives, as far as possible in working order, is not a new phenomenon. It began immediately some of the very earliest types were phased out of active life. Though only a very small number can ever now be restored and vast numbers have gone the way of all obsolete hardware over the last century and a half, steam locomotives have never gone to the breaker's yard or to solitary and protracted decay in some obscure corner of the railway system without regret on the part of those responsible. Nevertheless, the passing of steam from British Railways over the last ten years has added urgency to the existing enthusiasm of preservation societies and so it is likely that enough will survive not only to satisfy those who are actively interested but to provide an adequate historical record of a superseded form of motive power. Steam engines are not ideal objects for incarceration in museums, splendid and valuable though the work of railway museums is. They should be preserved not only in perfect condition but actually working.

By reason of its location and potentially its size as well, the Severn Valley line is particularly well equipped to play a leading part in this important field of industrial archaeology. Descriptions follow of the present collection of fourteen locomotives on the line and this will grow in both size and variety.

2-8-0, no. 8233

Sir William Stanier's 8Fs, introduced in 1935, became one of the most numerous and popular classes. Over 850 were built by the 'Big Four'

69

railway companies and by private builders as well. They survived to the very last days of steam operations on British Railways, often performing exceptionally arduous duties, such as hauling 1,000-ton limestone hopper trains from the Peak District.

No. 8233 was built by the North British Locomotive Co. in August 1940 at their Hyde Park works in Glasgow, destined for war service in France, but after the fall of France was delivered instead to the LMS. In 1941, like many others of her class, she was requisitioned for war service again and sent to Persia. After three years on the Trans-Iranian Railway, she was moved to the Suez Canal Zone and worked by the Egyptian State Railways until 1952 when the War Department brought her back to this country; following overhaul at Derby, she was used on the Longmoor military railway.

On return to British Railways, renumbered 48773, the engine was allocated to Polmadie depot, Glasgow, until withdrawn from service in 1962. In the following year she was reinstated after an overhaul and transferred to Carlisle, withdrawn again, but returned to spend her last years at Stockport (Edgeley) and Rose Grove depots. She had received a heavy intermediate overhaul at Crewe in 1966, including the fitting of a newly-overhauled boiler and was selected as the 8F in a condition most suitable for preservation. Eventually she was acquired by the Stanier 8F Locomotive Society and arrived at Bridgnorth on 4 January 1969, only 36,000 miles after the last overhaul. Since then, she has been restored as LMS no. 8233, and joined the exclusive ranks of preserved locomotives permitted to travel to BR Open Days.

2-6-0, no. 46443

No. 46443 is one of 128 class 2 MT tender locomotives built to the design of H. G. Ivatt, last chief mechanical engineer of the LMS. Twenty of them were completed under LMS auspices in 1946 and a further 108 by BR between 1948 and 1953, when the design was superseded by the very similar BR 78XXX class of 2-6-0s. The engines operated on all regions of British Railways except the Southern.

This example was built at Crewe and commissioned in February 1950. For over ten years she was shedded at Derby and worked on passenger trains, mainly to Burton, Nottingham and Birmingham until being moved to Saltley in 1961. Her last overhaul followed a collision with a diesel engine. In April 1967 she was purchased by

Richard Willcox, a member of the then Severn Valley Railway Society, and taken to Bridgnorth later that month.

2-6-0, no. 43106

Like no. 46443, this locomotive was one of a class designed by Ivatt for the LMS which was continued in the early years of BR. They were built at Doncaster and Darlington between 1947 and 1952. No. 43106 was completed at Darlington in April 1951.

The engine was shedded first at South Lynn on the Eastern region and subsequently at Woodford Halse, Saltley and Kingmoor (Carlisle). During her last two years, at Preston, she was slightly damaged in a derailment at Colne in April 1968, after which she was withdrawn and purchased by eighteen members of the Severn Valley Railway Society and installed at Bridgnorth in August 1968.

2-6-0, no. 46521

Another Ivatt 2 MT tender locomotive, although one of a slightly modified batch built after nationalization at Swindon, for service on the Western region, was finished in February 1953.

She was shedded first at Oswestry and then for over six years at Brecon, at one time the centre for a number of lines, in central Wales, and worked on passenger and freight services to Llanidloes, Hereford, Newport and Merthyr Tydfil. In October 1959 she was transferred to Oswestry and did similar duties to Welshpool, Ellesmere and Whitchurch, and in April 1963 moved to Machynlleth depot for service on the Pwllheli, Aberystwyth, Barmouth and Dolgellau lines. She was withdrawn in November 1966 and sent to Barry whence she was recovered by two members of the Severn Valley Railway for restoration to the Swindon green livery and to work on the line.

4-6-0, no. 45110

The Stanier class 5, known as the 'Black Stanier', was introduced in 1935 and over the following twenty years 842 examples were built. They were the backbone of the London Midland Region until the end of steam in 1968. No. 45110 was one of the third batch to be constructed and was completed at the Vulcan Foundry, Newton-le-Willows, in June 1935.

For twenty-nine years it was shedded at Holyhead and worked on

71

express passenger and freight trains to Chester, Birmingham, London, Manchester and Liverpool. In March 1964 she was moved to Stafford and used on freight services in the west Midlands. Steam operations ended at Stafford the following year when the engine was moved first to Bolton and later to Lostock Hall, Preston, from where she participated in the last scheduled steam operations on British Railways.

No. 45110 was purchased by a fund set up on the initiative of David Porter of the Flairavia Flying Club at Biggin Hill civil airport and moved to Ashford in Kent early in 1969 to be kept in the former BR shed there with three ex-Southern locomotives. Mr Porter later decided that its preservation days should be spent more actively and she was towed in goods trains from Ashford to Bridgnorth in August 1970. Once fully restored, she is to be named 'R.A.F. Biggin Hill', with LMS pattern nameplates.

2-6-4T, no. 80079

No. 80079 was one of 155 tanks built to a standard design under the direction of R. A. Riddles, chief mechanical engineer of BR at Derby, Doncaster and Brighton between 1951 and 1956, and derived from the Fowler, Stanier and Fairbairn 2-6-4 tanks first constructed under LMS auspices in 1930.

The Severn Valley engine was built at Brighton in March 1954 and shedded at Tilbury for service on the London, Tilbury and Southend line. On 30 January 1958 she was involved in the Dagenham East accident, colliding with a preceding train at 25 m.p.h. in thick fog, though she was not seriously damaged. On the electrification of the Fenchurch Street–Shoeburyness line in 1962, the engine was transferred to the Western region at Croes Newydd depot, Wrexham. In common with other Wrexham locomotives, she worked on the Severn Valley line during the last year of scheduled BR passenger services in 1962-3.

In July 1965 no. 80079 was sold to Woodham Bros of Barry and bought by a large group of Severn Valley members in 1970 for complete restoration and service on the line.

0-6-0, no. 3205

The 120 locomotives of Collett's 2251 class were used all over the GWR system after their introduction in 1930. No. 3205 was completed at Swindon in October 1946 and shedded at Gloucester for nine years for use on local passenger and freight workings to Ross, Hereford, Ledbury, Cheltenham and Swindon. For four years from 1956, the engine was shedded at Worcester and employed on banking duties between Honeybourne and Campden before its allocation to Shrewsbury for a year which included work on the Severn Valley line.

Her last years before withdrawal in June 1965 were spent on the SR line between Templecombe and Exeter after which she was bought by the 2251 Preservation Fund and restored at Buckfastleigh in 1965–6 by a small team led by Tony Goss. The custodian of the engine, David Rouse, was responsible for the decision to link the locomotive with the Severn Valley line and she was towed by diesel to Stourbridge in February 1967 whence she travelled under steam with four coaches to Bridgnorth on 25 March. No. 3205 was chosen to head the first public passenger train on the Severn Valley line on 23 May 1970.

0-6-0PT, no. 1501

This locomotive was the second of a batch of ten pannier tanks with outside cylinders completed at Swindon during the summer of 1949. The design originated under F. W. Hawksworth to a GWR order but no examples were built until after nationalization. They were mainly designed for heavy shunting, but in practice they were principally used for moving empty passenger stock. With several others of its class no. 1501 began work in this capacity between Old Oak Common and Paddington before being transferred to Southall in December 1950 where it remained on normal depot duties for ten years.

The advent of 350 h.p. diesel shunters rendered the 15XXs redundant unusually early and at the beginning of 1961 no. 1501, together with no. 1502 from Didcot and no. 1509 from Newport, was assembled at Swindon and sold to the National Coal Board for service at the Keresley colliery, Coventry. No. 1501 survived both its stablemates at Keresley and remained active there until September 1969. All three had been reserved for preservation by the Severn Valley and by the Warwickshire Railway Society. The other two were plundered for spare parts before being surrendered for scrap, while no. 1501 arrived at Bridgnorth in November 1970 for full restoration.

2-6-2T, no. 4566

This small Prairie tank was built at Swindon and entered service in October 1924. It was one of 175 engines constructed to G. J. Churchward's design in two batches, first at Wolverhampton in 1906–8 and then at Swindon from 1909 until 1929. They were very successful and became great favourites of the GWR for branch line work, including the Severn Valley line until the transfer of no. 5518 from Kidderminster in 1960.

No. 4566 served mainly in the south-west from Bristol and Penzance and has the distinction of being the last steam engine to be repaired at the Newton Abbot works in July 1959. After storage at Plymouth she was withdrawn in April 1962 and sold to Woodham Bros of Barry for breaking up. The engine lay there for seven years but in 1969 David Rouse and Bob Sim examined all the Prairies at Barry with a view to selecting one for possible purchase and use on the Severn Valley line. Apart from a number of missing fittings no. 4566 was found to be in surprisingly good condition and was consequently bought through a preservation appeal. She was towed to Bewdley in a succession of freight trains in August 1970, where full restoration, which is expected to take two or three years, is now in progress.

0-6-0T, no. 47383

The 'Jinty' tank was constructed for the LMS by the Vulcan Foundry, Newton-le-Willows, and entered service in October 1926. Its shunting and transfer trip work over a period of forty years was done from a number of sheds including Devons Road in East London, Chester, Carlisle, Burnley and Newton Heath, Manchester. She was first withdrawn at the end of 1966 but was returned to work at Williamsthorpe colliery, Chesterfield, for another year.

The initiative to purchase the 'Jinty' came from F. G. Cronin and B. H. Crick of Manchester, and the Manchester Rail Travel Society was formed to raise funds for the purchase of the engine in collaboration with the Severn Valley Railway. In the event she was bought as part of an Association of Railway Preservation Societies package deal and was moved to Bridgnorth by road in May 1967.

0-6-0T, no. 686, 'The Lady Armaghdale'

This six-coupled side tank locomotive was built by the Hunslet Engine Co. of Leeds in 1898 for service on the Manchester Ship Canal Railway. The engine was specially designed for work on that line which had many short radius curves. It was originally named 'St John' and worked continually on the MSCR, apart from overhauls at Leeds in 1938 and 1958 until it was withdrawn as surplus to requirements in 1963. However, it was immediately bought by I.C.I. for use at their Dyestuffs Division works at Blackley, close to the engine's former depot, where it was renamed 'The Lady Armaghdale' and worked transferring coal from the electrified Manchester–Bury line to the boiler house within the works.

In 1968, for reasons of economy, rail operations at the works were abandoned and the engine was offered for preservation. It arrived at Bridgnorth in July 1969 where, after minor repairs, it has been used for shunting and similar duties, normally alternating with the Manning Wardle described elsewhere.

0-6-0ST, no. 813

No. 813 is a typical example of the small fleet of 0-6-0 saddle tanks owned by the Port Talbot Railway Co. and used for shunting and coal traffic on their system in South Wales. It was built by Messrs Hudswell and Clarke of Leeds in 1901 and allocated to Duffryn Yard depot, which was absorbed by the GWR in 1908. Early in 1934 she was bought by Beckworth Collieries Ltd of Northumberland where the engine worked until 1967.

The fund to save her was launched by P. H. Goss and the purchase completed in August 1967 ready for delivery to Bridgnorth by road in November.

0-6-0ST, no. 2047, 'Warwickshire'

No. 2047 was the last locomotive to be built by the Leeds firm of Manning Wardle, which went into voluntary liquidation in 1927 after sixty-eight years of engine building She was ordered by the Rugby Portland Cement Co. in April 1926 and delivered to their New Bilton works in August that year.

Initially the engine worked hauling special wooden-framed tippler wagons of cement ore on the very steep line between the quarry and

75

Severn Valley Railway Locomotives

	3205 GWR 2251 Class 0-6-0 Collett goods	46443 LMR Ivatt 2MT 2-6-0	2047 Manning Wardle 0-6-0ST Rugby Portland Cement	813 Hudswell Clarke 0-6-0ST GWR & Port Talbot Rly no. 26	47383 LMSR Fowler 3F 0-6-0T Jinty	1738 Peckett 0-4-0ST CEGB Hams Hall no. 4	43106 LMR Ivatt 4MT 2-6-0	8233 LMSR Stanier 8F 2-8-0 Ex-48773	686 Hunslet 0-6-0T ICI Blackley 'Lady Armaghdale'	45110 LMSR Stanier 5MT 4-6-0	4566 GWR 45XX Class 2-6-2T Churchward small Prairie	1501 WR 15XX Class 0-6-0PT Hawksworth O/C pannier	46521 LM-Type Ivatt 2MT 2-6-0	70000 BR Class 7MT 4-6-2 'Britannia'
Tractive effort (lb)	20,155	17,410	12,695	17,410	20,835	15,230	24,170	32,438	15,940	25,455	21,250	22,515	18,510	32,150
Working pressure (lbf/in²)	200	200	160	160	160	160	225	225	160	225	200	200	200	250
Weights (tons–cwt) full Engine	43–8	47–2	30–0	44–0	49–10	29–0	59–2	72–2	35–0	70–6	57–0	58–4	47–2	94–0
Tender	36–15	37–2					40–6	53–13		53–13			37–2	49–3
Total	80–3	84–4	30–0	44–0	49–10	29–0	99–8	125–15	35–0	123–19	57–0	58–4	84–4	143–3
Empty Engine	40–0	43–5	25–0	41–10	38–6	24–0	55–4	65–15	29–0	63–11	49–15	47–2	43–5	85–3
Tender	17–9	19–14					20–10	26–15		26–15			19–14	23–3
Total	57–9	62–19	25–0	41–10	38–6	24–0	75–14	92–10	29–0	90–6	49–15	47–2	62–19	108–6
Dimensions (ft in): Length: Engine	28–7¾	30–5¼	25–0	30–9	31–4¾	23–5	32–2½	37–11	24–0	38–6	36–4½	33–0	30–5¼	44–1
Tender	25–0½	22–8½					22–8½	25–1¾		25–1¾			22–8½	24–8
Total	53–8¼	53–1¾	25–0	30–9	31–4¾	23–5	55–11	63–0¾	24–0	63–7¾	36–4½	33–0	53–1¾	68–9
Coupled wheelbase	15–6	13–9	10–0	13–3	16–6	5–6	15–4	17–3	10–3	15–0	11–6	12–10	13–9	14–0

Total wheelbase	40–0$\frac{3}{4}$	44–1	10–0	13–3	16–6	5–6	46–11$\frac{3}{4}$	52–7$\frac{3}{4}$	10–3	53–2$\frac{3}{4}$	26–10	12–10	14–1	58–3
Maximum width	8–8	8–7$\frac{1}{2}$	7–10	8–7	8–9	8–2	8–8	8–7$\frac{11}{16}$	7–11	8–7$\frac{5}{8}$	8–9$\frac{1}{4}$	8–11$\frac{1}{2}$	8–7$\frac{1}{2}$	8–8$\frac{3}{4}$
Maximum height	12–8$\frac{7}{16}$	12–5$\frac{3}{4}$	11–0	12–5	12–6%	11–8	12–10	12–10	11–7$\frac{1}{2}$	12–8	12–9$\frac{9}{16}$	12–6$\frac{1}{8}$	12–5$\frac{3}{4}$	13–0$\frac{1}{2}$
Height to boiler C.L.	8–1	8–3	6–2	6–7$\frac{1}{2}$	7–4$\frac{1}{4}$	5–8$\frac{1}{2}$	8–11	8–11	6–2$\frac{1}{2}$	8–9	7–9	7–8	8–3	9–4
Pony wheel diameter		3–0					3–0	3–3$\frac{1}{2}$		3–3$\frac{1}{2}$	3–2		3–0	3–0
Driving wheel diameter	5–2	5–0	3–6	4–0$\frac{1}{2}$	4–7	3–2$\frac{1}{2}$	5–3	4–8$\frac{1}{2}$	3–5	6–0	4–7$\frac{1}{2}$	4–7$\frac{1}{2}$	5–0	6–2
Tender wheel diameter	4–1$\frac{1}{2}$	3–6$\frac{1}{2}$					3–6$\frac{1}{2}$	4–3		4–3			3–6$\frac{1}{2}$	3–3$\frac{1}{2}$
Boiler: Small O.D.	4–5$\frac{1}{8}$	4–3	3–6	4–0	4–2	4–11	4–9$\frac{1}{8}$	5–0	4–0	5–0	4–2	4–5$\frac{1}{8}$	4–3	5–9
Large O.D.	5–0$\frac{1}{2}$	4–8	Parallel	4–1	Parallel	Parallel	5–3	5–8$\frac{3}{8}$	Parallel	5–8$\frac{3}{8}$	4–9$\frac{1}{2}$	5–0$\frac{1}{2}$	4–8	6–5$\frac{1}{2}$
Length between tubeplates	10–3	10–10$\frac{1}{2}$	8–8	9–6	10–10$\frac{3}{4}$	9–6	10–10$\frac{1}{2}$	12–3$\frac{1}{2}$	8–0	13–3	10–6	10–3	10–10$\frac{1}{2}$	17–0
No. of tubes & O.D.	218–1$\frac{5}{8}$	162–1$\frac{5}{8}$	115–2	176–1$\frac{3}{4}$	194–1$\frac{3}{4}$	124–1$\frac{3}{4}$	160–1$\frac{5}{8}$	202–1$\frac{3}{8}$	160–1$\frac{7}{8}$	151–1$\frac{7}{8}$	196–1$\frac{5}{8}$	176–1$\frac{5}{8}$	162–1$\frac{5}{8}$	136–2$\frac{1}{8}$
Tube heating surface (ft^2)	1,069	924	521	793	967	540	1,090	1,479	648	1,479	992	1,245	924	226 4
Grate area (ft^2)	17·4	17·5	9·6	13	16	9$\frac{1}{4}$	23	28·6	10·8	28·6	16·8	17·4	17·5	42
Firebox heating surface (ft^2)	102	101	55·6	79	97	63	131	171	31	171	95	102	101	210
No. of flues & O.D. (in)	6–5$\frac{1}{8}$	12–5$\frac{1}{8}$	None	None	None	None	24–5$\frac{1}{8}$	21–5$\frac{1}{8}$	None	26–5$\frac{1}{8}$	6–5$\frac{1}{8}$	None	12–5$\frac{1}{8}$	40–5$\frac{1}{2}$
Superheating surface (ft^2)	76	134					231	230		348	78		134	677
Total evaporative surface (ft^2)	1,171	1,025	576	872	1,064	603	1,221	1,650	679	1,650	1,163	1,347	1,025	2,474
Mechanical: Cylinders (2) dia. × stroke (in)	17$\frac{1}{2}$ × 24	16 × 24	14 × 20	16 × 24	18 × 26	14 × 22	17$\frac{1}{2}$ × 26	18$\frac{1}{2}$ × 28	15$\frac{1}{2}$ × 20	18$\frac{1}{2}$ × 28	17 × 24	17$\frac{1}{2}$ × 24	16$\frac{1}{2}$ × 24	20 × 28
Piston valve dia. × travel (in)	Slides	8 × 5$\frac{15}{16}$	Slides	Slides	Slides	Slides	10 × 6$\frac{7}{16}$	10 × 6$\frac{1}{2}$	Slides	10 × 6$\frac{1}{2}$	Slides	8 × 6	8 × 5$\frac{15}{16}$	11 × 7$\frac{3}{4}$
Valve gear type	Stephenson	Walschaerts	Stephenson	Stephenson	Stephenson	Stephenson	Walschaerts	Walschaerts	Stephenson	Walschaerts	Stephenson	Walschaerts	Walschaerts	Walschaerts
Tender: Water capacity (gals)	3,000	3,000	630	900	1,200	920	3,500	4,000	750	4,000	1,000	1,350	3,000	4,250
Coal capacity (tons)	5	4	1	2	2$\frac{1}{4}$	8 cwts	4	9	1	9	3$\frac{3}{4}$	3$\frac{1}{4}$	4	7

GVS

the crushing plant and for this reason was fitted with 'dumb buffers'. Apart from a short period at the Southam works in 1943 she remained at New Bilton until superseded by a conveyor system at the quarry in the early 1950s. Thereafter she worked on dwindling coal traffic from the main line into the works until the end of 1966.

The cement company, wishing to see the locomotive preserved, offered her for sale at the very modest price of £150 which was enthusiastically accepted and the engine transported by road to Bridgnorth in October 1967. Since then, she has been completely overhauled and named 'Warwickshire' to commemorate forty years' work in the county.

0-4-0ST, no. 1738

This engine was built in 1928 by Peckett & Sons at the Atlas Locomotive Works, Bristol, and delivered later that year to Hams Hall power station at Coleshill. Pecketts built very little other than small saddle tanks for industrial use and no. 1738 is a typical example of their W6 class of which over forty were constructed between 1926 and 1940. Her work, together with that of an identical engine at Hams Hall, consisted of the transfer of coal wagons from the exchange sidings of the then LMS at Coleshill to the power station boilers. Later the two Pecketts were relegated to feeding the older 'A' station which in its later years was only used in winter and thus the engines spent a part of each year in store.

In 1968 the 'A' station was closed altogether and the fleet of steam engines displaced by diesels. No. 1738 was bought by a regular driver at Bridgnorth, J. McNally, and delivered for immediate operation in July 1968.

4-6-2, no. 70000, 'Britannia'

The first major locomotive to be built to the sole design of BR, 'Britannia' was completed at Crewe in 1951 as a 'Pacific' class. From Stratford, Brighton and Crewe she worked the heaviest main-line expresses and in 1952 hauled the funeral train of King George VI from Sandringham. To save her from the breakers' yard, a group of enthusiasts bought her in 1970 and leased her to the Severn Valley Railway Co. She arrived at Bewdley in April 1971 and is housed at Bridgnorth.

78

10
Steam Nostalgia

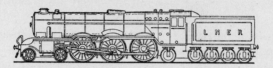

The passing of steam on British Railways and the substitution of diesel and electric traction coincided in the 1960s with the onset of the steam locomotive preservation movement. It has been gathering momentum ever since. So numerous have the preserved steam locomotives become that the Worcester Locomotive Society which 'exists to cater for the interests of all average railway locomotive enthusiasts throughout Great Britain' published in the autumn of 1970 a *Preserved Locomotives Checklist* by R. M. Pritchard, listing in great detail all known steam locomotives in Britain. The origin, type and location of these locomotives are catalogued and described. It is a very valuable survey of the activities of the locomotive preservation movement, covering several hundred items. Some are owned privately, some by industrial concerns, some by the railway preservation companies, others by museums, by British Railways on the Vale of Rheidol line, and by the two splendid independent narrow-gauge railways – the Romney, Hythe & Dymchurch Railway and the Ravenglass & Eskdale Railway – which have operated for many years.

As the *Standard Gauge Standard*, published by the Standard Gauge Steam Trust, wrote in 1970, in its first issue:

Serious railway preservation began in the Midlands, in October 1950 – when the first of all the ideas for saving a railway came to fruition in the formation of the Talyllyn Railway Preservation Society. Since that time Midlands' men have been prominent in the field, but until comparatively recently there has been no activity in the five Midlands' counties. It began in 1964, when the Whitehouse/Garland engines, destined for the Dart Valley Railway in Devon, began to arrive at Tyseley and later, in January 1966, when No. 7029 'Clun Castle' took up residence at the steam shed there.

What glorious days those were, when the little 2-6-2 tank No. 4555 ran scheduled passenger trains to Knowle & Dorridge out of Snow Hill, resplendent in Great Western livery, and in September 1965 took a train out over the Severn Valley line to Alveley. We wondered then just how the infant Severn Valley Railway Society would fare and shook our heads over the obstacles which they would have to surmount.

The year 1966 saw 'Clun' working specials out of Snow Hill. She went as far North as Shrewsbury and was seen regularly on the trip freights to Banbury. Over the winter of 1966/67 she was repainted – it took five men working five days a week three months to do the job – and in March 1967, No. 7029 ran those epic specials on the last trains to Chester and Birkenhead the weekend before the electrified train service to Euston began. It was the near failure of the engine (due to a valve spindle connection to the rocker arm stripping) that made us realise the need for a team to be built up if she was to continue running, and from it sprang the organisation behind 7029 Clun Castle Ltd. and later the Standard Gauge Steam Trust. But it was 1967 which provided the major thrills.

It all started over lunch in the Officers' Mess at Paddington when Gerry Fiennes, who had just vacated the Chair of the Western Region Board for the Eastern, suggested some runs out of King's Cross and in spite of difficulties which sprang up daily, these actually came off. Before she left for Peterborough where she was stabled, 'Clun Castle' had her motion rebushed and other light repairs undertaken, and she was run in on the Knowle & Dorridge to Banbury car trains. On the Eastern she never let us down for a second and made trips to Carlisle, Leeds, York and Newcastle becoming the most travelled of all her class.

Then came the steam ban on BR and preserved steam from the Midlands had to take a new look at itself. Out of the re-thinking came the tremendous organisation at Tyseley – it was an ill wind that blew, but the proverb held true.

80

Midland centres for steam locomotives at Tyseley (Standard Gauge Trust) and at Bridgnorth (Severn Valley Railway) prospered and grew rapidly after scheduled steam-hauled services on British Railways ended in 1968.

A preserved steam locomotive, inert and motionless in a museum or exhibited on a railway platform, as the 'Locomotion' is at Darlington, is a historical relic and an object of nostalgia to older generations: a locomotive steaming, running, hauling and speeding at the head of a train becomes an exciting, glamorous, pulsating and living mechanism, beloved by men and women of all ages. Such is the attraction of the major steam preservation lines, so widespread has the preservation movement become, that there is now an Association of Railway Preservation Societies (ARPS) for co-ordination and organization of the railway preservation movement, including a campaign to operate, by 1975, steam locomotives again on special trains on British Railways; the loan of preserved locomotives by public authorities to preservation societies; terms of purchase of locomotives for preservation society members; the publication of a journal entitled *Railway Forum* and many other associated steam preservation matters. The ARPS already has more than seventy members including such diverse bodies as

The Bahamas Locomotive Society
The East Anglian Locomotive Preservation Society
The Ivatt Locomotive Trust
The Lakeside Railway Society
The Dowty Railway Preservation Society
The Bulleid Pacific Preservation Society
The Crewe Transport Museum Trust
The Corris Society
The Great Western Society
H. P. Bulmer Limited.

These, and other societies, mostly own steam locomotives and rolling stock, and include those lines operating under Ministry of Transport Light Railway orders, such as the Severn Valley, Dart Valley, Worth Valley, Bluebell and other standard-gauge and narrow-gauge railways. All this indicates the wide interest and varied character of the preservation movement. It deserves to be encouraged. No public funds are entailed; the railway preservation explosion is entirely privately owned and financed.

The growth of tourism, national and international, will prove a special and enduring market with remarkable growth prospects for the railway preservation companies. Visitors from home and abroad may well be expected to fortify the claim of the companies that they represent an important national asset, capable of developing into outstanding features of the tourist and allied leisure industries.

The Dart Valley Railway

This is probably the first of the preservation lines to achieve commercial and financial viability and to become a major tourist feature in the 'Glorious Devon' so well publicized by the GWR for over a hundred years. Originally the Buckfastleigh, Totnes & South Devon Railway, promoted by local interest and worked by the South Devon Railway which was taken over by the Great Western in 1868, the BT&SD Railway was not taken over itself by the Great Western until 1897. The 9¼ miles of track was built in the broad gauge and converted to standard gauge in May 1892. The traffic on the line was largely agricultural and partly from local textile mills and, of course, there was always a good volume of tourist trade on the line, serving such romantic Devonian towns and villages as Ashburton, Buckfastleigh and Totnes. The original project, with I. K. Brunel as the engineer, was conceived in 1845, at the height of the railway mania and the Bill was passed in 1848. All this occurred at very much the same time as the birth of the Severn Valley Railway and the two lines both suffered a long and turbulent period of gestation. Eventually, shortened to 9 miles 20 chains, it opened on 1 May 1872, ten years after the Severn Valley Railway. It was closed to passengers on 3 November 1959 and to goods on 10 September 1962, thus completing just over ninety years in operation. Nearly seven years later (to be precise, on 21 May 1969), a commercial company, the Dart Valley Light Railway Company, which had been formed for the purpose some years earlier, reopened the line with support from the Dart Valley Association formed in 1966. Today, this railway operates in one of the most gorgeous of the Devon valleys and as its passenger traffic receipts show, has already become a major tourist attraction greatly enhanced by fine Great Western steam traditions, as the following locomotive inventory demonstrates:

ex-GWR 2-6-2T, no. 4555, Churchward, built Swindon 1924
ex-GWR 2-6-2T, no. 4588, Churchward, built Swindon 1927
ex-GWR 0-4-2T, no. 1420, Collett, built Swindon 1933
ex-GWR 0-4-2T, no. 1450, Collett, built Swindon 1935

ex-GWR 0-6-0T pannier, no. 1369, Collett, built Swindon 1934
ex-GWR 0-6-0 pannier, no. 6412 ⎫
             no. 6430 ⎬ Collett, all built at
             no. 6435 ⎭ Swindon 1934–7
ex-BR 0-6-0T, no 1638, Hawksworth, built Swindon 1951
ex-BR (Collett GW design) 4-6-0, no. 7827 'Lydham Manor', built
Swindon 1950
Peckett saddle tank, former contractor's engine 0-4-0ST, built 1942

These are all representatives of a unique collection of former Great
Western locomotive types well within the memory of millions of
railway travellers. The Dart Valley Railway with its strong GWR
links and background, in traditional Great Western country and
holiday haunts, has a most promising future.

The Keighley & Worth Valley Railway

This line was opened in 1867, closed to passengers on New Year's
day 1962, and to goods later the same year. It was reopened by the
present company, entirely privately financed, in 1968. It claims
today to have the largest collection of steam engines and stock of any
of the preservation companies in Britain and operates from its own
platform at Keighley (BR) station, over 4¾ miles to Oxenhope. The
line is an ideal place to see and hear steam locomotives hard at work
as it climbs all the way to Oxenhope. The section just outside
Keighley station is 1 in 58. The whole of the line is actually situated
within the boundary of the West Riding borough of Keighley, but
the urban part of the town is left at Ingrow (1¾ miles up the branch),
where the line passes through a 125-yard tunnel. From then on the
scenery is typical of much of the West Riding: stone-built villages
with their mills interspersed with stretches of rather bleak countryside. Above Haworth and Oxenhope, the last two stations on the
line, rise the moors made famous in the novels of the Brontë sisters
who lived at Haworth Parsonage.

Originally built by local land- and millowners, the line was worked
by the Midland Railway until the local company was absorbed in
1886 and between 1884 and 1955 a part of the line was used by
Great Northern Railway Keighley to Bradford trains. After absorption into the LMSR in 1923 and into the London Midland region of
British Rail in 1948 it finished its nationalization days in the North
Eastern Region of British Railways.

83

The following assembly of motive power, led by former BR locomotives, is impressive:

0-6-0T	no. 1708	Johnson, Midland Railway, built Derby 1880
0-6-0	no. 3924	Fowler, Midland Railway, built Derby 1920
0-6-0ST	no. 751	Barton Wright, L&YR, Beyer Peacock, built 1881
0-6-0	no. 957	Barton Wright, L&YR, Beyer Peacock, built 1887
0-4-0ST	no. 51218	Aspinall, L&YR, built Horwich 1901
0-4-0ST	no. 19	Aspinall, L&YR, built Horwich 1910
0-6-2T	no. 4744	Gresley, GNR, built North British Loco. Co. 1921
0-6-2T	no. 52	Riches, Taff Vale, built Neilson 1889
2-6-0	no. 13000	Hughes Fowler, LMSR, built Horwich 1926
4-6-0	no. 45212	Stanier, LMSR, built Armstrong Whitworth 1935
0-6-0T	no. 5775	Collett, GWR, built Swindon 1929
0-6-0T	no. 72	(USA), SR, built U.S. Transport Corp. 1943
0-6-0T	no. 69023	'Joem', Worsdell, LNER, built Darlington 1951
2-6-2T	no. 41241	Ivatt, LMSR, built Crewe 1949
2-6-4T	no. 80002	BR, built Derby 1951
0-6-0WT	'Bellerophon', Haydock 1874	
0-6-0ST	'Sir Berkeley', Manning Wardle 1891	
0-4-0ST	'Lord Mayor', Hudswell Clarke 1893	
0-6-0T	Hudswell Clarke 1903	
0-6-0T	Hudswell Clarke 1919	
0-6-0ST	'Isabel', Hawthorn Leslie, 1919	former
0-4-0ST	no. 1999 Peckett 1941	contractors'
0-4-0ST	no. 2226 Barclay 1946	locomotives
0-6-0ST	no. 57 Stephenson 1950	
0-6-0ST	no. 62 Stephenson 1950	
0-6-0ST	no. 63 Stephenson 1954	
0-6-0ST	'Fred' Stephenson, 1945	
0-6-0	'Harlaton', Barclay 1941	

This list excludes the Stanier 'Black 5', owned by Mr W. E. C. Watkinson, described later under the Strathspey Railway, and a collection of former Midland, Great Northern, Lancashire & Yorkshire, North Eastern, Great Western and British Rail coaches and goods wagons. The Keighley & Worth Valley Railway is an adventurous and excellent project, and I prophesy a great future for it.

The Strathspey Railway

From the West Riding we travel to the north-east of Scotland, to a line called the Strathspey Railway, to be opened shortly, in a country long famous for stock-breeding, whisky and tourism, and also in recent years for winter sports, based in the near-by Cairngorms. The line is 5 miles long from Aviemore to Boat of Garten. The history of the line is of much interest. Originally, it was part of the Inverness & Perth Junction Railway and was opened in 1863. The line was promoted by the Highland lairds, including the Earl of Seafield who owned all the land in the area. The railway provided much improved transport for the timber from the large plantations on the Seafield estate, and timber remained an important source of freight traffic. In 1865 the I&PJR became part of the Highland Railway. In 1866 the rival Great North of Scotland Railway reached Boat of Garten from the north, and the station became the junction for the GNSR's Speyside line which passed through the 'whisky country' of the valley, to the north of Grantown-on-Spey. In the nineteenth century the Aviemore–Boat of Garten line was part of the main route to Inverness and the northern Highlands, but in 1898 a new and shorter route from Aviemore to Inverness was opened and the line through Boat of Garten assumed secondary importance. Nevertheless, the line carried a vast amount of traffic during the two world wars.

On reopening shortly, under the new title of the Strathspey Railway, the company is strongly supported by the Scottish Railway Preservation Society and the Highlands and Islands Development Board. The Scottish Railway Preservation Society (SRPS) has built up a large and interesting collection of Scottish locomotives, carriages and wagons at its depot at Falkirk and many items suitable for operating the railway will be moved to Aviemore. It is also hoped to purchase the $7\frac{1}{4}$ miles of trackbed from Boat of Garten to Grantown-on-Spey for possible relaying in the future, and to build a railway museum at Boat of Garten.

The railway starts at Aviemore and the station will be to the north of the BR station, close to the four-road locomotive shed which will house the line's engines and carriages. The railway runs along the Spey valley between the Monadhliath Mountains to the west and the

85

Cairngorms, the Mecca for ski-ing enthusiasts, to the east. In spite of
the impressive views of the mountains from the railway the actual
course of the line is fairly level. Approaching Boat of Garten, it
passes through a coniferous plantation. Boat of Garten, a village
which has grown up since the coming of the railway, is two miles
from Loch Garten, well known as the scene of the ospreys' return to
Britain.

Here on the Strathspey Railway will run the beautifully restored
Stanier 'Black 5', no. 5025, at present on short-term loan to the
Keighley & Worth Valley Railway. No. 5025 is owned by Mr
Watkinson of Hanley Swan, Worcester, a leading preservationist and
a champion of the steam locomotive crusade in Britain today. This
engine, bought from British Railways and thoroughly overhauled, as
new, and better, by the Hunslet Engine Co. of Leeds, is a peerless
example of a class which will immortalize the name of Sir William
Stanier, F.R.S., for so many years chief mechanical engineer of the
London Midland & Scottish Railway, and promises to be the
cynosure of all eyes on the Strathspey Railway. It will excite the
envy of locomotive lovers everywhere.

In addition to no. 5025, originally built by the Vulcan Foundry in
1934, Strathspey expect to operate:

ex-North British 0-6-0, no. 673 'Maude', built Neilson 1891
ex-Caledonian 0-4-4T, no. 419 McIntosh, built St Rollox 1907
0-6-0T, no. 20   } both built Barclay 1939
0-4-0ST, 'Dailuaine'}

together with many former Caledonian, Highland, GNSR, GSWR,
LMSR and BR coaches and wagons.

North Yorkshire Moors Railway

Of special antiquarian and historical allure is the line from Grosmont
to Ellerbeck, say 6¾ miles, later to go on possibly to Pickering, 18
miles in all, now called the North Yorkshire Moors Railway. As part
of the early Whitby & Pickering Railway it was opened in 1836. It
was horse-worked but there was a 1,500-yard incline from Grosmont
to Beck Hole. Coaches and wagons were hauled up this by a rope
wound round a horizontal drum and attached at the other end to a
water tank wagon. The water was emptied at the foot of the incline
and the tank wagon hauled back by descending Whitby-bound
coaches and wagons. Later a stationary steam engine was used. In

1845 the Whitby & Pickering Railway was bought by George Hudson's York & North Midland Railway which relaid the line for locomotive working, except for the Beck Hole incline. The incline was closed on 1 July 1865 after a 4-mile deviation south of Grosmont was built, which included a new station at Goathland. In addition to the usual traffic of a farming area there was stone from local quarries and at one time there were ironworks at Grosmont, although all traces of them have disappeared today. The line passed to the LNER in 1923 and the North East Region of British Railways in 1948. The Grosmont–Pickering line was closed completely on 8 March 1965.

The North Yorkshire Moors Railway Preservation Society (NYMRPS), which was formed in 1967, aims to reopen the whole route from Grosmont to Pickering. The first contract, already signed, covers the trackbed from Grosmont to Pickering, lineside buildings and the rails from Grosmont to Ellerbeck. Negotiations are going ahead to see if it is possible to purchase the remaining rails through to Pickering. The NYMRPS works in close co-operation with the North Eastern Locomotive Group which owns the two NER engines on the line and is to build an engine shed at Grosmont. The Hull & Barnsley Railway Stock Fund has provided two coaches of the Hull & Barnsley Railway for use on the restored line. At open weekends members of the society are allowed to travel on the line and it is hoped to obtain a Light Railway Order in the near future.

The NYMR has its own section of Grosmont station. Immediately on leaving the station the line passes through a 120-yard-long tunnel; the smaller tunnel alongside now used as a footpath was used by the original horse worked trains. The railway runs at the bottom of the valley of the Murk Esk for most of the way to Goathland, the headquarters of the line. At Ellerbeck the three massive spheres of Fylingdales Early Warning Station come into view and the railway passes through one of the bleaker parts of the North Yorkshire moors, running through Fen Bog before striking wooded Newtondale which it follows until reaching the northern end of the Vale of Pickering. This North Yorkshire enterprise on the moors is a fascinating attempt to revive one of the earliest passenger lines. Motive power is impressive:

ex-NER 0-8-0	no. 63395	Built Darlington 1918
ex-LNER 0-6-0	no. 2392	Worsdell, built Darlington 1923
ex-LNER 2-6-0	no. 62005	Peppercorn, built Darlington 1949

ex-LMSR 4-6-0	no. 5428	Stanier, 'Eric Treacy', Armstrong Whitworth 1937
0-6-2T	no. 29	Kitson 1904
0-6-2WT	no. 5	Stephenson 1909
0-4-0WT	no. 3	Borrows 1898
0-4-0WT	'Salmon'	Barclay 1942
0-4-0ST	'Mirvale'	Hudswell Clarke 1955

and the rolling stock on the NYMR is a miscellany of Hull & Barnsley Railway, LNER and BR origin.

The Bluebell Line

Famous, and deservedly so, among the steam railways revived in recent years is the 4¾ miles from Sheffield Park to Horsted Keynes in Sussex called the Bluebell line: originally opened in 1882, the line was built as part of the 20-mile Lewes–East Grinstead Railway (LEGR), controlled and backed by the London Brighton & South Coast Railway (LBSCR), which took over the LEGR as soon as the latter had been completed. As well as local passengers, the line carried a certain amount of through traffic from the south coast to London, thus avoiding the busy Brighton–London main line. On the freight side, there was general agricultural traffic, especially milk for London and timber. The line passed to the Southern Railway in 1923 and BR (Southern Region) in 1948. It was closed on 28 May 1955, but it was discovered that the closure was illegal and BR had to reopen the railway on 7 August 1956, with the minimum service of four trains each way required in the LEGR Act. The line was closed for the second time on 17 March 1958, but part of it was reopened in August 1960.

The publicity surrounding the line led to the formation of a preservation society which negotiated a lease of the section from Sheffield Park to Horsted Keynes (the track south of Sheffield Park, and north of Horsted Keynes was subsequently lifted). This was the first preservation society to operate a passenger service on a standard gauge railway. Because of its relatively early start the Bluebell Railway acquired a number of interesting locomotives and carriages, mainly from the railways of southern England. For the first year the northern terminus of the Bluebell was Bluebell Halt, outside Horsted Keynes station, but later on the trains ran into the main line station, and indeed became the sole users of it after the electric service from

Haywards Heath to Horsted Keynes was withdrawn on 28 October 1963. The Bluebell has now purchased its line from British Railways.

The headquarters of the Bluebell line are at Sheffield Park, near the National Trust's Sheffield Park Gardens, where the locomotive shed and museum are situated. The line runs through the gentle and attractive country of the mid-Sussex weald and is at its best in the spring when there are masses of bluebells, primroses and other spring flowers. The station at Horsted Keynes is impressive with an atmosphere of the late Victorian period.

The steam traction of the Bluebell line is magnificent and of great interest to railwaymen everywhere precisely because the Bluebell was the first of the standard gauge preservation lines in Britain. It had a good deal of choice in the purchase of locomotives:

ex-LBSCR	0-6-0T	no. 72	'Fenchurch'	Stroudley	built Brighton 1872
ex-LBSCR	0-6-0T	no. 55	'Stepney'	Stroudley	built Brighton 1875
ex-LBSCR	0-6-2T	no. 473	'Birch Grove'	Billington	built Brighton 1898
ex-LSWR	4-4-2T	no. 488		Adams	built Neilson 1885
ex-SECR	0-6-0T	no. 178	'Pioneer II'	Wainwright	built Ashford 1910
ex-SECR	0-6-0T	no. 27		Wainwright	built Ashford 1910
ex-SECR	0-6-0T	no. 323	'Bluebell'	Wainwright	built Ashford 1910
ex-SECR	0-6-0T	no. 592		Wainwright	built Longhedge 1901
ex-NLR	0-6-0T	no. 2650		Park	built Bow 1880
ex-GWR		no. 3217	'Earl of Berkeley':		
			'Dukedog'	Collett	built Swindon 1938
ex-BR	4-6-0	no. 75027	BR Standard		built Swindon 1951

0-40-T, 'Captain Baxter' Fletcher Jennings 1877 ⎫
.0-6-0ST24, 'Stanford' Avonside 1927   ⎬ ex-contractors'
2-2-0WT, 'The Blue Circle' Aveling & Porter 1926' ⎭ locomotives

These fourteen locomotives and passenger stock and wagons were drawn from the London, Brighton & South Coast Railway, the South Eastern & Chatham Railway and the London & South Western Railway.

The Lochty Railway

Back in Scotland, there is the Lochty private railway in Fife, covering just 2 miles from Lochty to Knightsward. It opened for freight in 1898 and was closed in 1964 as uneconomic. Then, after BR had lifted the tracks, a local farmer, John Cameron, formed the Lochty Railway Co. and obtained a Light Railway Order. The line was reopened, to passenger traffic only, on 14 June 1967 and the company owns a single steam engine, the former LNER Pacific by Gresley, built at Doncaster in 1937, numbered 60009 and named 'Union of South Africa'. It operated on the east coast route from London to Edinburgh and from Aberdeen to Glasgow and now hauls on the Lochty line one of the two observation cars used on the Coronation Express and then in the fifties and sixties on the most beautiful west Highland route to Fort William and Mallaig. The Pacific locomotive hauling the single observation car on the Lochty Railway is a stirring sight for all those who loved the east coast expresses, King's Cross to Waverley and beyond, in the days of steam.

The North Norfolk Railway

No brief survey of steam preservation lines in the standard gauge would be complete without a reference to what is happening in the northern part of Norfolk – the creation of a steam venture between Sheringham and Weybourne, a distance of about $2\frac{3}{4}$ miles. This line was opened in 1887 as part of the Cromer to Melton Constable line and was built by the Eastern & Midlands Railway (East&MR), which ran into grave financial difficulties in 1893 when the Midland and Great Northern Joint Railway (M&GNJR) was formed to take it over. During the eighties and nineties of the last century the 'Poppyland' area of Norfolk was becoming, as indeed it still is, very popular as a holiday coast with numerous excellent resorts on the dryer side of England, and in the M&GNJR days the line carried through trains from King's Cross and Manchester to Cromer. The railway led to the growth of the town of Sheringham. In contrast, traffic at the rather isolated Weybourne station, opened on 1 July 1901, did not develop as the M&GNJR had anticipated. Being a joint railway, the line was unaffected by the grouping, except that the owning companies were now the LMSR and the LNER. From 1 October 1936 operation of the line was undertaken by the LNER, and the M&GNJR's locomotives and rolling stock was taken over by that company. The railway remained jointly owned until nationalization, when it became part of the Eastern Region. The Cromer–Melton Constable line survived the closure of most of the old M&GNJR system in 1959, but the line between Sheringham and Weybourne was closed to passengers on 6 April and to goods on 28 December 1964.

The North Norfolk Railway (NNR), supported by the local preservation society, plans to reopen the line from Sheringham (still served by trains from Cromer) to Weybourne, with the possibility of relaying the track west of Weybourne in the future. The NNR already owns the track from Sheringham to Weybourne and intends purchasing the land and buildings from BR when the Ministry of Transport grants a Light Railway Order. Finance for the reopening of the line has been raised by issuing shares to the public. This line starts from Sheringham BR station and after leaving the town runs within sight of the cliffs of the north-east Norfolk coast. To the south lies heath and woodland. There are several embankments on the line, but it is generally an easy and flat route without engineering difficulties. In addition to a variety of rolling stock, generally pre-1923 grouping in origin, the NNR owns a number of steam locomotives, including:

ex-GER   0-6-0, no 65462, Worsdell, Stratford 1912

ex-LNER   (GER) Holden 4-6-0, no 61572, Beyer Peacock 1928

and three tank engines of varying vintages and origins. The flavour of this preservation line is definitely Great Eastern, Liverpool Street, Stratford and 'Norfolkman'.

The Little Railways of Wales

The five narrow-gauge steam-operated passenger-carrying railways in Wales are of great historical and contemporary interest and no survey of steam preservation in the 1970s can be complete without a description of these lines.

	Length	Gauge	First opened
Festiniog Railway	$9\frac{3}{4}$ miles	1 ft $11\frac{1}{2}$ in	1836
Vale of Rheidol (BR)	$11\frac{3}{4}$ miles	1 ft $11\frac{1}{2}$ in	1902
Welshpool & Llanfair	$4\frac{1}{4}$ miles	2 ft 6 in	1903
Snowdon Mountain Railway	$5\frac{3}{4}$ miles	(2 ft $7\frac{1}{2}$ in rack)	1896
Talyllyn Railway	6 miles	2 ft 3 in	1866

The Festiniog Railway

This line opened for slate trains on 20 April 1836 and ran only from the quarries at Blaenau Festiniog to Portmadoc where the slates could be taken away by sea. The line, to the narrow gauge of 1 foot $11\frac{1}{2}$ inches, was constructed with a falling gradient from Blaenau so that the loaded trains could coast down by gravity to Portmadoc, and then the empty wagons after discharge of the slates were hauled back by horse. Because of great traffic increases during the first quarter century of the railway's life, steam traction was inaugurated in 1863. Even then the loaded slate trains ran down by gravity but the steam locomotives hauled the empties back up the bank, and to augment revenue the passenger service was introduced in January 1865. Slate traffic continued to grow, and the fleet of

91

steam locomotives to expand, but within fifty years, changes in building fashions and designs caused serious decline in the slate quarrying industry of North Wales and the line was closed to passengers on 16 September 1939, shortly after the outbreak of World War II, and eventually closed to freight traffic, including slates, on 2 August 1946. Not for long though, for in 1954 control of the line passed to the doyen of steam locomotive preservationists, Alan Pegler, now known internationally as the owner of the 'Flying Scotsman'. After reconstruction and re-financing of the company, reopening progress was rapid: from Portmadoc to Boston Lodge on 23 July 1955; to Minffordd on 19 May 1956; to Penrhyndeudraeth on 30 March 1957; to Tan-y-Bwlch in April 1958 and to Ddualt, a total length of 9¾ miles, on 6 April 1968.

The Festiniog Railway Co., powerfully supported by the Festiniog Railway Society, has turned a moribund railway into a thriving concern, now carrying more than 300,000 passengers annually. The line starts at Portmadoc Harbour on the Caernarvonshire coast, although it is mostly in Merioneth; the trains run along the 'Cob', a one-mile length of embankment built early in the nineteenth century across to Glaslyn Estuary, to Boston Lodge, where the company works are situated, and then starts the climb to Ddualt, crossing the Pwllheli branch of British Railways at Minffordd and into wider and more impressive scenery. The Cei Mawr, a 60-foot high dry stone embankment, is memorable for all passengers and then follow severe curves to Tan-y-Bwlch, for many years the terminus of the reopened Festiniog Railway. In recent years the trains have travelled through the Garnedd tunnel to Ddualt, an isolated station without road access. Much of the line between Ddualt and Blaenau has been submerged as part of the electricity pumped storage scheme, but work has already begun on a new railway deviation which will carry the line to Blaenau again.

The locomotive inventory on page 93 is unique.

Together with these ten locomotives is passenger stock derived from the Welsh Highland and Lynton & Barnstaple Railways, now closed.

'Prince', built in 1863, is the oldest steam locomotive working scheduled passenger services in Britain today, and a little senior to London's oldest inhabitant, a lady born in 1864. The Double Fairlies, 0-4-4-0 wheel arrangement, built respectively in 1879 and 1885, are still very much in service and both are maintained at the company's works at Boston Lodge where they were originally built. Famous British locomotive builders, such as the Hunslet Engine Co. of Leeds

'Jinty' tank no. 47383 (ex-LMSR no. 7383). Owned by the Manchester Rail Travel Society and sold previously by BR to the N.C.B., this fine specimen was moved to the Severn Valley Railway in 1968 from the Williamsthorpe colliery, Chesterfield. *Above:* on the M1 motorway in Nottinghamshire in May 1968. *Below:* shunting in the colliery sidings, August 1967.

Ex-GWR 1500 class shunting engines. Created just pre-nationalization, these powerful six-coupled pannier tanks weighed 58 tons 4 cwt and carried 3 tons 6 cwt of coal and 1,350 gallons of water. *Above:* no. 1501, owned by the Warwickshire Industrial Locomotive Preservation Group, at Bridgnorth for renovation. This fine engine was rescued from the Keresley colliery of the N.C.B. in November 1969 and will be operational on the Severn Valley line in 1972. *Below:* no. 1500 (the first of her class) at Swindon in May 1949.

'Warwickshire', a Manning Wardle 0-6-0 saddle tank built in 1926, formerly owned by the Rugby Portland Cement Co. Ltd, now belonging to the Warwickshire Industrial Locomotive Preservation Group, and brought to the Severn Valley Railway in 1970. *Above:* after naming at Bridgnorth, 30 August 1970. *Below:* crossing Oldbury viaduct with a works train in 1970.

'The Lady Armaghdale', a Hunslet side tank 0-6-0 no. 686, built 1898. Formerly owned by the Manchester Ship Canal Co. Ltd and then by I.C.I. Ltd, she arrived at Bridgnorth for the Severn Valley Railway in 1970. She now belongs to the Warwickshire Industrial Locomotive Preservation Group. *Above:* at Bridgnorth, 30 August 1970. *Below:* at Oldbury Grange with a works train, later the same day.

The world record under steam. Nigel Gresley A3 Pacific named
'Mallard', ex-LNER no. 4468, now BR no. 60022 preserved in the
Clapham Railway Museum, achieved 126 m.p.h. down Stoke Bank on
the East Coast route to Scotland on 3 July 1938 with a test train of
240 tons including dynamometer car. *Above:* on Leeds–London
express in 1964. *Below:* on Tees–Tyne Pullman leaving Kings Cross
in 1965.

Bridgnorth station. *Left: c.* 1863, from the Castle. *Right: c.* 1890, from Pudding Hill.

Dinner at Evesham to celebrate the opening of the Oxford, Worcester & Wolverhampton Railway 1 May 1852.

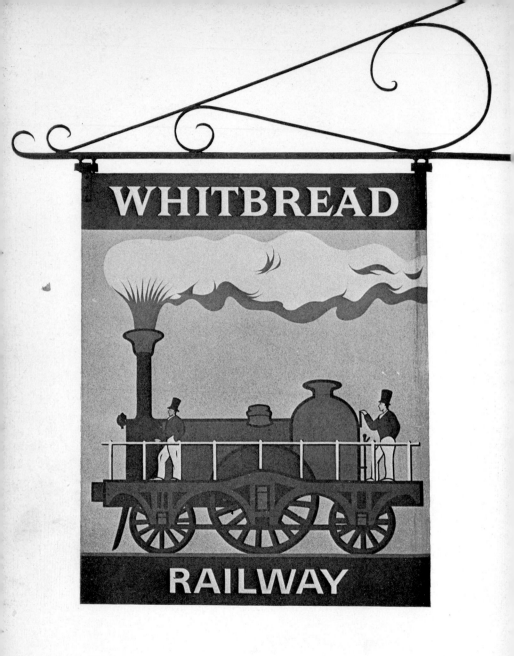

Pub sign at Evesham.

Above: North Yorkshire Moors Railway open weekend at Goathland station. *Left to right:* ex-NER 'Raven' 0-8-0, formerly BR no. 63395, built Darlington in 1918; ex-NER 0-6-0ST no. 29, built by Stephenson in 1904; 0-6-0ST 'Salmon' built by Barclay in 1942. *Below:* tank engines at Croes Newydd (Wrexham, Denbighshire) in 1968. 0-6-0PT BR Hawksworth no. 1638, built at Swindon in 1951, is now fully operational on the Dart Valley Railway. Ex-GWR Collett 0-6-2 no. 6651 was scrapped shortly after this photo was taken.

Above: '"Dukedog" at dusk' – ex-GWR 4-4-0 no. 3217, named 'Earl of Berkeley' (one of a class of thirty), stands at Sheffield Park on the Bluebell line. *Below:* the 'Union of South Africa', ex-LNER Gresley Pacific 4-6-2 no. 60009 built at Doncaster in 1937 at Lochty on the Lochty Private Railway in Fife, Scotland.

Keighley & Worth Valley Railway. *Above:* ex-BR Ivatt 2-6-2T
no. 41241 built at Crewe in 1949 heads the special train to reopen the
line from Keighley to Oxenhope on 29 July 1968. The second engine
is 0-6-0T no. 72 built by the Vulcan Ironworks in the USA for the US
Army Transportation Corps and purchased by the Southern Railway
in 1946. *Below:* on loan to the Keighley & Worth Valley Railway
and destined for the Strathspey Railway, no. 5025, 'the finest of the
Stanier Black Fives', was built by Vulcan for the LMSR in 1934.
She is now owned by W. E. C. Watkinson, Esq.

'Great Western glory' at Hereford in 1971. *Above:* no. 5786, a doyenne of the Swindon pannier tanks and finest preserved specimen of her GWR class, now owned by the Worcester Locomotive Society. *Below:* 'King George V', no. 6000, the Collett masterpiece of the 1920s in BR livery, now owned by Bulmers of Hereford.

The Vale of Rheidol Railway – the only BR narrow-gauge line, and the only BR steam traction. *Above:* no. 9 leaving Aberystwyth. *Below:* 2–6–2T 'Prince of Wales' built by Davis & Metcalfe in 1902 approaching Aberffwrd.

The Dart Valley Railway. *Above*: ex-GWR 0-4-2T no. 1420 built at Swindon in 1933 crossing the River Dart with an auto-trailer. *Below*: 0-6-0 pannier tank no. 1369 with outside cylinders heading an ex-GWR train at Buckfastleigh station before carnival celebrations at Ashburton. *Right*: 0-6-0 pannier tank no. 6412 with inside cylinders approaching Buckfastleigh, near Caddaford.

Welshpool & Llanfair Light Railway, 2 feet 6 inch gauge. 0-8-0T no. 10, 'Sir Drefaldwyn', near Llanfair Caereinion.

Above: Talyllyn Railway, 2 feet 3 inch gauge. 0-4-0WT no. 2, 'Dolgoch', in Dolgoch Woods.   *Below:* Festiniog Railway, 1 foot 11½ inch gauge. Double Fairlie 0-4-4-0, 'Earl of Merioneth', near Ddualt.

0-4-0ST	no. 1	'Princess'	England	1863	
0-4-0ST	no. 2	'Prince'	England	1863	
0-4-0ST	no. 5	'Welsh Pony'	England	1867	
0-4-0ST		('Blanche')	Hunslet	1893	ex-Penrhyn
2-4-0ST		('Linda')	Hunslet	1893	Quarry Railway
2-6-2T		'Mountaineer'	Alco (USA)	1916	ex-Pithiviers Tramway, France
0-6-0ST		—	Peckett	1944	
0-4-4-0T	no. 3	'Earl of Merioneth'	Fairlie	1885	Boston Lodge
0-4-4-0T	no. 10	'Merddin Emrys'	Fairlie	1879	Boston Lodge
0-4-4-0T		—	Beyer Peacock	1909	ex-Tasmanian Government Railways

(which renovated no. 5025 LMS Stanier 'Black 5' for the Strathspey Railway), Beyer Peacock and Peckett, have contributed to the Festiniog tractive power, though it is the Fairlie and Beyer Peacock double-enders which steal the thunder, especially as the latter was undoubtedly the precursor of the notorious 2-6-6-2 Beyer Peacock Garrett locomotives which appeared in 1927 to work the very heavy mineral trains from the East Midland coalfield to London, on the old Railway main line. The Double-Fairlies merit closer study; because the average gradient on the line was 1 in 92 and the steepest 1 in 60 and the curves between 2 and 4 chains, Fairlie was commissioned to design these double-ended locomotives. In February 1870 the first severe trials were held with 'Little Wonder', a locomotive of 0-4-4-0 wheel arrangement; the outcome was sensational. A train of 72 wagons, 648 feet long (an enormous length on a narrow-gauge railway), with a gross weight, including the engine, of 206 tons, was hauled up an incline of 1 in 85 at 5 m.p.h. By comparison the 'Welsh Pony's' best performances on these trials, with 150 lb steam pressure against 'Little Wonder's' 200 lb, was twenty-six wagons and a weight, including the engine, of 74 tons. Thus Fairlie's system of double-engines gained credence for working steep gradients and was much employed elsewhere. Suffice to say two of these 0-4-4-0 engines, vintages 1879 and 1885, persist to this day on the Festiniog Railway.

The Vale of Rheidol Railway

The company opened the 11¼ miles of line, narrow gauge 1 foot 11½ inches throughout, for goods traffic in August 1902, and for passenger traffic on 22 December 1902. Eleven years later it was absorbed by the Cambrian Railway and depended for rail access on the Cambrian main line, Welshpool, Moat Lane Junction, Dovey

Junction to Aberystwyth, Strata Florida, Lampeter and Carmarthen. The valley offered both freight, notably agricultural products, and good tourist prospects from the developing seaside resort of Aberystwyth, but the goods traffic was soon to evaporate, first the lead ore and timber, and by the twenties all freight traffic. The Vale of Rheidol became a Great Western line in 1923 when the Cambrian was taken over and today it is a unit of British Railways, having been nationalized as part of the GWR in 1948. It is BR's only steam operated and narrow-gauge passenger service. There are three locomotives:

no. 9	'Prince of Wales'	Davies and Metcalfe	1902
no. 8	'Llyweln'	GWR Swindon	1923
no. 7	'Owain Glyndwr'	GWR Swindon	1923

These are all of 2-6-2T design, and the carriages are GWR built.

The scenery on the line is splendid, especially around Devil's Bridge, where Wordsworth wrote of the waterfall in 1824:

How art thou named? In search of what strange land,
From what huge height, descending? Can such force
Of waters issue from a British source,
Or hath not Pindus fed thee, where the band
Of Patriots scoop their freedom out, with hand
Desperate as thine? Or come the incessant shocks
From that young Stream, that smites the throbbing rocks,
Of Viamala? There I seem to stand,
As in life's morn; permitted to behold,
From the dread chasm, woods climbing above woods,
In pomp that fades not; everlasting snows;
And skies that ne'er relinquish their repose;
Such power possess the family of floods
Over the minds of Poets, young or old!

The railway today uses the BR station at Aberystwyth and across a platform width may be seen a modern diesel and the 2-6-2T of the 1902 'Prince of Wales' heading the train up the vale to Devil's Bridge. She runs out of the station past the former standard-gauge locomotive shed which has now been adapted to house Vale of Rheidol engines and carriages, and then regains the pre-1968 route. For the first 4 miles to Capel Bangor it runs along the floor of the Rheidol valley, but then starts the climb to Devil's Bridge. The line reaches a ledge out on the rock, from where there are spectacular views of the river in the valley below, and the hills across the valley. The section just before Devil's Bridge is particularly impressive. Devil's Bridge is a small village, with the beauty spots of the Devil's Punchbowl and the Mynach Falls near by.

Welshpool & Llanfair Light Railway

Also on the former Cambrian Railways territory is the Welshpool & Llanfair Light Railway, 2 feet 6 inches gauge, opened in 1903 on land largely given by local owners, notably the Earl of Powis, and originally linking Welshpool to the small Montgomeryshire town of Llanfair Caereinion, population about 1,400, where the present head-quarters of the railway are situated. The railway runs close to the River Banwy for two miles before turning into a side valley and crossing the rebuilt Banwy Viaduct. There is a six-arch stone viaduct over the River Cwmbaw, Brynelin Viaduct, which is the chief engineering work on the line. Castle Caereinion, the present terminus, is reached through pleasantly undulating countryside. Unlike many Welsh narrow-gauge railways, the Llanfair line had no connection with the slate quarrying industries. The freight carried included farm produce and livestock, while coal was transhipped from the standard-gauge wagons at Welshpool and brought up the line. Until the 1930s stone was also carried a short distance from a quarry on the outskirts of Welshpool down to the main line station there. The W&L was worked by the Cambrian Railway which was absorbed by the GWR in 1922, and the W&L Co. itself was taken over by the GWR the next year. On account of uneconomic operation the line was closed to passengers in 1931, and twenty-five years later the line closed to freight. The preservation company which partially reopened the line on 6 April 1963 (a blessed day on the calendar for reopening railway lines), is directly controlled by its members; there is only one paid member of the staff – the general manager. Not long after reopening, one of the piers of the Banwy Viaduct was seriously damaged by floods, but it was replaced and the line over the viaduct was reopened 10 months later on 16 August 1965. The company hopes to reopen the further 3¾ miles of track from Castle Caereinion to the outskirts of Welshpool. The last mile of track through Welshpool to the main line station has been lifted. 'The Earl' and 'The Countess', the railway's two original locomotives, have returned to the lines, after being placed in storage following BR's complete

95

closure in 1956. The original W&L passenger coaches were scrapped in 1936, but the preservation company has secured coaches from the Admiralty's Chattenden & Unor Railway in Kent: also from the Zillertalbahn in Austria. Also from Austria comes a locomotive (no. 10) built in France during World War II for German military use, later used on the Styrian Government Railway in Austria. Here are the six locomotives:

0-6-0T	no. 1	'The Earl'	Beyer Peacock	1902
0-6-0T	no. 2	'The Countess'	Beyer Peacock	1902
0-4-0T	no. 5	'Nutty'	Sentinal	1929
0-4-4-0T	no. 7	'Monarch'	Bagnall	1953 (articulated)
0-4-0WT	no. 8	'Dougal'	Barclay	1946
0-8-0T	no. 10	'Sir Drefaldwyn'	SFB France	1944

Snowdon Mountain Railway

The Snowdon Railway, although not strictly a preservation line, deserves mention if only as the sole rack-railway in Britain. It is 2 feet $7\frac{1}{2}$ inches gauge and $5\frac{3}{4}$ miles long, opened in 1896 and in continuous operation ever since. Without any signalling system (unnecessary in view of conditions), the line climbs to 3,540 feet above sea level. All five engines are of 0-4-2T wheel arrangement. The need for the 'racking' is evident from gradients of 1 in $5\frac{1}{2}$, and speeds are, of course, relatively very slow, the ascent or descent taking about an hour, in coaches giving reasonable weather protection to travellers and sightseers. So popular is the line in summer that a half-hourly service is maintained, facilitated by pass loops for the trains at three points on the journey. The Snowdon Mountain Railway is certainly a tourist attraction but very worth while and useful, without which few would enjoy the views of sensational beauty on clear days from the summit of Snowdon.

Talyllyn Railway

This is one of the epics of the steam preservation era, now operated as a viable commercial concern. It runs six miles from Towyn to Abergynolwyn and opened on 13 November 1866, four years after the Severn Valley Railway. The line (2 feet 3 inches gauge) starts on the Towyn (Wharf) station on the Merioneth coast and runs inland and uphill. At Towyn (Pendre) are the company's works and carriage sheds. The line then runs into the Fathew Valley, and after three miles it reaches the hillside which it keeps to for the rest of the journey. The mountain of Cader Idris dominates much of the scenery, and the charmingly situated station of Dolgoch must be one of the most photographed railway scenes in Wales, when the engines take water there. Abergynolwyn station is high above the village and scenery is impressive on the line throughout, and spectacular on the further mile of line beyond Abergynolwyn which should carry its first passenger trains within four or five years. Originally, the railway was built by the owners of the Bryneglwys slate quarry to transport their slate to the standard-gauge line at Towyn. The line also carried passengers for most of its length. Passenger trains terminated at Abergynolwyn, but slate trains ran on a further mile and the trucks were then hauled up the first of two inclines to the quarry. In 1911 control of the quarry and the railway passed to Sir Haydn Jones, M.P. for Merioneth, who kept his promise that the railway would continue to operate in his lifetime, even after the Bryneglwys Quarry closed in 1948. This was only achieved, however, by putting off urgent renewals of equipment. In 1950 Sir Haydn died and it seemed inevitable that the railway would be closed.

Then, the first Talyllyn Railway Preservation Society (TRPS) was formed and through the generosity of Sir Haydn's executors secured control of the line. The TR, alone among the preserved railways, can thus boast: 'We never closed.' The railway was in a very parlous state when the TRPS took over, but since then much has been achieved. The line is now completely re-laid. Major repairs have been carried out to bridges, and the stations at Towyn (Wharf) and Abergynolwyn have been rebuilt. Now that the line is in first-class order, work has started on bringing the disused section along the Gwernol valley beyond Abergynolwyn, formerly used by slate trains, up to passenger standards. The two original locomotives, 'Talyllyn' and 'Dolgoch', have been completely rebuilt. Two more engines were purchased from the neighbouring Corris Railway. This 2 feet 3 inches gauge line from Machynlleth to Aberllefni was laid in 1858 as a horse tramway. Steam locomotives were used from 1879 until the closure of the line in 1948. Another two engines were taken over from industrial use. In 1951 the TR had only four coaches; the bodies of others from the Corris and Glyn Valley lines have been rebuilt, and in recent years completely new bogie coaches have been built to the company's designs. The locomotive inventory on page 98 is attractive. There is also 0-4-0WT no. 7, 'Irish Pete', 3 feet gauge, Barclay 1949, rebuilding to 0-4-2T, 2 feet 3 inches gauge, which completes the total of six locomotives.

0-4-2ST	no. 1	'Talyllyn'	Fletcher Jennings	1865
0-4-0WT	no. 2	'Dolgoch'	Fletcher Jennings	1866
0-4-2ST	no. 3	'Sir Haydn'	Hughes	1878
0-4-2ST	no. 4	'Edward Thomas'	Kerr Stuart	1921
0-4-0WT	no. 6	'Douglas'	Barclay	1918

But the line nearly closed, and the epic of how it was saved from the scrap-heap has been told with eloquence, spirit and candour by Mr L. T. C. Rolt in *Railway Adventure*, first published in 1953 (with an admirable foreword by Sir John Betjeman), which relates the history of Talyllyn from the first extant time-table of 1867 to the general managership of Sir Henry Haydn Jones from 1911 to 1950. The leadership and prudence of Mr Patrick Garland, a director of the Talyllyn Railway Co., chairman of the Dart Valley Railway Co., consultant to the Severn Valley Railway Co. and steam railway preservationist extraordinary, has been the salvation of Talyllyn, aided by the selfless devotion of hundreds of enthusiasts who have laboured unremittingly for twenty years without reward, other than the great personal and individual satisfaction of running an efficient and picturesque line.

Of course, the 15-inch gauge railways, namely the Ravenglass & Eskdale, 7 miles long in the Lake District, converted from 36-inch gauge in 1915, and the Romney, Hythe & Dymchurch Railway in Kent, 13¾ miles long, may now, or very soon will be, regarded as preservation lines, though not in quite the same sense as the other historic railways described in this chapter. They are both of great scale model interest and value, toys on a utilitarian and imaginative scale, rather than historical relics. Yet both operate on commercial lines, if not with uniformly good financial results.

The accolade for steam locomotives preserved and operated for posterity will go today, early in the seventies, to four great engines: 'City of Truro', exhibited in the Great Western Museum at Swindon and steamed very occasionally for special trains on the Western Region of British Railways, when she fills every viewer with pride and nostalgia for the day, nearly seventy years ago when she took the Ocean Mails down Wellington Bank in Somerset, en route for Bristol and Paddington at the world's then record speed of 102 m.p.h.; 'King George V', Great Western no. 6000, preserved at Bulmers in Hereford, the western terminal of the Four Cities line, route of the famous Cathedrals Express (London to Oxford, Worcester and Here-

98

ford); the Gresley A3 Pacific no. 4472, 'Flying Scotsman', which hauled London & North Eastern expresses, and later worked on British Railways until she was bought and operated with such conspicuous success by Mr Alan Pegler, chairman of the Festiniog Railway, who combines with a sense of adventure, deep love of steam engines and our great railway heritage; and finally the Severn Valley Railway's BR class 7 no. 70000, 'Britannia'.

Note on Sources

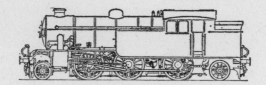

The history of the Severn Valley Railway has never been written in detail before and thus I have had to rely mainly on unpublished sources.

The British Railways Historical Records at 66 Porchester Road, London, W.2., contain:

Minutes of Board Meetings: vol. 1, 1852–3; vol. 2, 1853–61; vol. 3, 1861–71.

Minutes of Shareholders Meetings, 1853–73.

Minutes of the Finance Committee, 1853–4.

File of Board Papers, 1864–73.

Printed Shareholders Address Book, 1870.

Contract for the building of the line with Brassey, Peto and Betts, dated 26 May 1858.

File of certificates of payments to contractors, 1859–64.

Copy of draft contract with the OW&W, 1857.

Printed copy of the agreement with the GWR for the modification of its lease on the Severn Valley line, dated 1 September 1865.

Ledger, 1853–9.

Ledger, 1859–71.

Journal, 1858–71.

Cash Book, 1852–63.

Cash Book, 1864–8.

The Record Office, House of Lords, contains the deposited plans, books of reference and associated documents for the Severn Valley

Railway Bills of 1853, 1855 and 1856; and the minutes of evidence of both Lords and Commons Select Committees on the 1853 and 1855 Bills, and the Commons minutes of evidence on the 1856 Bill.

The County Record Offices of Shropshire and Worcestershire contain material similar to that at the House of Lords only on a local level.

Contemporary newspapers are invaluable because they reflect the prejudices, hopes and doubts of the time as well as providing factual information. However, the extent to which complete sets have been preserved varies a great deal and for this reason I have had to rely mainly on the *Worcester Herald*, *Evesham Journal*, *Bridgnorth Journal*, *Shrewsbury Chronicle*, *Eddowes Salopian Journal* and the *Kidderminster Shuttle*. Unfortunately, the *Illustrated London News* had lost most of its interest in railways by the time the Severn Valley line was begun. The *Railway Times* published items about it from its origins until its final absorption by the GWR; *Bradshaw's Shareholders' Guide*, *Railway Manual and Directory* contained an entry about the line every year over the same period.

There are very few books which have any bearing on the Severn Valley line at all. Even E. T. MacDermot's *History of the Great Western Railway* (ed. C. R. Clinker, vol. 1, 1833–63, Ian Allan, 1964), although unequalled for background material, contains very little detailed information about the origins and building of the line. Other published works worth consulting are:

J. Simmons, *Some Railway Schemes in the West Midlands 1833–65* (Railway Club, 9 September 1937).

C. R. Clinker, *Railways of the West Midlands: a chronology 1808–1954* (Stephenson Locomotive Society, 1954).

T. C. Tuberville, *Worcestershire in the 19th Century* (Longmans, 1852), pp. 150–164.

J. E. Norris, *The Railways of Worcester* (Railway Club, September, 1953).

G. Measom, *Guide to the Great Western Railway* (Griffin, 1860).

J. Randall, *Handbook to the Severn Valley Railway* (privately published, 1863).

The Severn Valley, Handy Aids Series, no. 7 (GWR, 1924).

Most of the individuals directly concerned in the building of the line have been included either in the *Dictionary of National Biography* or *Boase's Modern English Biography.* Relevant full-length biographies are: *The Life of Sir John Fowler,* by Thomas Mackay (John Murray, 1900), *The Life and Labours of Mr. Brassey,* by Arthur Helps (Bell, 1872) and *Sir Morton Peto, a Memorial Sketch* (Elliot, Stock, 1893).

Index

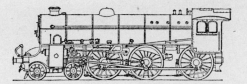

103

Preston, Lostock Hall, 72
Pritchard, John, 51
Pritchard, R. M., 79
Pwllheli, 71, 92

Quatford, 29

Railway Preservation Societies, Association of, 74, 81
Railways, economic & social effects, 12–14, 18
Rastrick, John, 33
Rattery bank, 62
Ravenglass & Eskdale Railway, 79
Rea, River, 51
Reading, 14
Reed, Charles, 16
Reed, William, 15, 16, 18
Reform Club, 26
Rheidol, *see* Vale of Rheidol
Riddles, R. A., 72
Robertson, Col. J. R. H., 67
Romney, Hythe & Dymchurch Railway, 79
Ross-on-Wye, 73
Rouse, David, 73, 74
Rufford, Francis, 11
Rugby Portland Cement Co., 75

Sabrina, 2
'Saint' class, 60
'St John', 75
Saltley, 70, 71
Seafield, Earl of, 85
Severn, River, 2, 45, 49, 51; origin of name, 2–3; uncertain navigation, 17, 20, 23–4, 26–7
Severn Valley Railway: Acts, 24–5, 27, 29-30, 67; Bills withdrawn, 27, 29, 31, 32
Severn Valley Railway Co., 65, 66, 68, 81
Severn Valley Railway Society, 65, 71
Shelburne, Lord, 45
Sheringham, 90
Sherriff, A. C., 40, 45, 46, 47
Shrewsbury, 2, 15, 16, 19, 21, 24, 25, 29, 37, 39, 42, 43, 44, 45, 50, 52, 57, 58, 73; enquiry, 67–8
Shrewsbury & Birmingham Railway, 21, 57
Shrewsbury & Chester Railway, 21, 37

Shrewsbury Chronicle, 16
Shrewsbury & Hereford Railway, 21, 25, 29, 51, 57
Shrewsbury Race Course Co., 21
Shrewsbury, Wenlock & Bridgnorth turnpike, 21
Shropshire, 1, 15; coalfield, 23; County Council, 66, 68
Shropshire Union Railways & Canal Co., 14, 41
Shuttleworth, George Edmund, 24
Sim, Bob, 74
Simmons, Capt., 11
Smirke, Robert & Sydney, 26
Smith & Knight, 30
Snowdon Mountain Railway, 91, 96
Somerset Central Railway, 24
South Eastern Railway, 14, 17, 26
South Lynn shed, 71
Southall, 73
Stafford, 72
Stafford Union Railway, 58
Staffordshire & Worcestershire canal, 48, 52
Standard Gauge Standard, 79–80
Standard Gauge Steam Trust, 79, 80, 81
'Stanley Baldwin', 61
Stanier 'Black 5', 71, 84, 86, 93
Stanier 8F Locomotive Society, 70
Stanier, Sir William, 69, 72, 86
'Star' class, 60
Stephenson, Robert, 8, 14
Stikeman, Henry, 20
Stirling, Patrick, 59
Stockton & Darlington Railway, 1
Stoke Prior, 42
Stour, River, 36
Stourbridge, 73
Stourport-on-Severn, 3, 10, 23, 30, 35, 36, 39, 43, 48, 49, 52, 54, 56, 62, 63; power station, 52, 57
Stratford-on-Avon, 42
Strathspey Railway, 84, 85–6
Sutton Bridge junction, 25, 29, 39, 65
Swindon, 58, 59, 60, 62, 71, 73

Talyllyn Railway, 91, 96–8
Tan-y-Bwlch, 92
Telford, Thomas, 4, 5
Teme, River, 51
Templecombe, 73